Christian
Writer's Coach

How to get the Most out of a
Writers Conference

By

the Northwest Christian Writers Association

Northwest Christian Writers Association
PO Box 2706
Woodinville, WA 98072-2706
http://www.nwchristianwriters.org

Copyright © 2013

Scripture quotations are from *The Holy Bible: The New International Version*, copyright ©1978 by the International Bible Society. Used by permission of Zondervan Bible Publishers.

For ordering information,
please contact *www.nwchristianwriters.org/cwc*

Cover & Interior Design by AudioInk Publishing
www.AudioInk.com

Northwest Christian Writers Association

The Christian Writer's Coach: How to get the most out of a writers conference

p. cm.

ISBN: 978-1-61339-488-5

1. LANGUAGE ARTS & DISCIPLINES / Publishing
2. LANGUAGE ARTS & DISCIPLINES / Authorship
3. LANGUAGE ARTS & DISCIPLINES / Composition & Creative Writing

For further information, contact the Northwest Christian Writers Association at (206) 659-9038 or president@nwchristianwriters.org

Endorsements

What others are saying about
the Christian Writer's Coach

"Having taught at dozens of writers' conferences at which newcomers had no idea what they should have brought with them or what they should be doing, this book is a solution to a major communication problem. Its focus on editors, pitches, teaching sessions, and networking makes it a must-have volume for anyone involved in freelance writing."

–Dr. Dennis E. Hensley author, *How to Write What You Love and Make a Living at it*

"Getting your book published is a marathon, not a sprint. This book helps you prepare for one of the refreshing stops along the way, where you also learn a lot about the road ahead and how to navigate it. Practical aids like this book expand your learning capacity."

– Les Stobbe, Literary Agent,
Author, and veteran of the publishing industry

"You want to take your writing aspirations beyond the next level? Get this book. Conferences can be a huge key to launching a writing career and this book will help you get the most of the ones you go to. Wish this had been around when I jumped into the world of publishing."

– Bestselling author James L. Rubart

"As an editor I've always made my best connections at conferences. Every beginning writer should attend conferences, and even long-time attenders will glean vital instruction here. There's no money better spent to prepare, to get the most out of it, and to learn how to leap ahead of the pack than from the industry professionals brought together in this excellent guide."

– Mick Silva, Editor, Coach, & Storyteller @ YourWritersGroup.com

"What I like about this book is that it's written by writers who are sharing their experiences with other writers. Great advice."

– Judy Bodmer, Director of Northwest Christian Writers Renewal and author of *When Love Dies: How to Save a Hopeless Marriage* and *What's in the Bible for Mothers*

"Who doesn't need a writer friend experienced in Christian publishing? Better yet, an experienced writer friend who will stay by your side all year round? With The Christian Writer's Coach, you get useful, practical, insider tips from 15 accomplished (read published) writer friends. They come alongside and deliver the goods in a straightforward style that is easily referenced time and again. Be prepared. Be productive. Get Coached!"

– Clint Kelly Novelist, Conference Speaker, Communications Specialist www.clintkellybooks.com

Acknowledgements

Every great project succeeds because great people pour themselves into it. We owe a debt of gratitude to the authors and the incredible editorial staff who made this book a success.

We thank Kim Martinez, Mindy Peltier, Lesley McDaniel, Delora Buoy, Marlene McCurley, and Agnes Lawless who spent countless hours acquiring and editing each article; and the extensive group of people who helped with promotion.

The editorial team is grateful to the Northwest Christian Writers Association for tasking us to develop this book. We have learned so much, including how to think as a group, organize the writing process, and finalize a manuscript.

We have experienced God's miraculous provision and life-giving refreshment as each of us faced real life issues and wanted to stop. During those times, we found the rest of the team willing and able to pick up the baton and keep working.

We'd like to thank the five authors who granted interviews for the biography section, and also thank the host of cheerleaders who wrote endorsements, listened to our frustrations, and cheered us on.

We also offer our appreciation to Brian and DeeDee at AudioInk Publishing, who put up with a host of questions, an avalanche of emails, and quietly added their expertise to turn our rough manuscript into a polished product.

Our passion and prayer for this book is to equip Christian writers to fulfill their calling and use their gift for the glory and honor of our Lord and Savior Jesus Christ. To Him be the glory and honor. Selah.

Table of Contents

Foreword

I remember the night that I showed up at my first meeting of a Christian writers group. I had completed a novel I knew was ready for publication. In fact, I expected that I'd soon sign a book contract, be able to quit my day job, and devote my life to writing.

I learned a few things in my first few months as part of the group:

1. My novel was *not* ready for publication.

2. Most published authors had one thing in common—a day job.

3. I was part of a faith community that would help me navigate that long and winding road toward my goal of publication.

An important part of my writing journey has been participation in conferences. At these events, I've learned about the craft and the publishing industry from experts. I've connected with other talented people of faith who believed in my work and encouraged me, and in turn I've been able to encourage and help them. I also met the person who became my agent as well as published authors who have become fans of my work.

Another important part of conferences is developing contacts. As a hiring manager for technology companies, I have dug through hundreds of resumes to pick the right person to interview for a single position. People that I met or knew personally had a definite advantage in the job-hunting process. Editors or agents face a similar challenge as they dig through stacks of query letters or manuscripts sent to them by people they've never met. Being able to meet these decision makers face-to-face gives you a chance to make a positive impression and stand out from the three-foot-deep slush pile. Today, the person who gets an agent or a book contract without first connecting personally is a relative rarity.

What I've learned as part of this faith community helped me get published in international, secular, and Christian magazines. I've advanced enough to become a member of the staff and faculty of our local conference so I can help others achieve their goals. What I've learned about the craft also helped me take my novel from not even *close* to being ready for publication to being a semifinalist and finalist in international competitions.

In this book you'll learn from best-selling authors and talented amateurs about the importance of conferences and how to prepare so you get the most out of your participation. You'll learn to approach the event with realistic expectations and goals. You'll hear writers who have achieved their goals of publication as well as those, like me, who know that it's prayer, persistence, and patience that will lead to that first contract.

We seek to influence the world for Jesus Christ, not for our own purposes. Part of becoming persons of influence is connecting with our faith community through conferences.

Dennis Brooke
President, Northwest Christian Writers Association
Storyteller and pre-published novelist

Introduction

Why in the world do we need another book on writing? Most writers have an ever-expanding library of books on the craft. Therefore, it is important to understand what value this book will add to your library before you hit the "buy" button.

The *Christian Writers' Coach*: *How to Get the Most Out of a Writers Conference* is the first in a series of books specially designed by Northwest Christian Writers Association writers. It is our goal to give you best-practices information and to put tools in your tool belt to help you succeed as a writer. You will find all of the links mentioned in this book at http://www.nwchristianwriters.org/Conferences.

We started this book with five bios of successful people in the industry. People who started out just like you and are making it in the world of publishing.

This book is designed as a primer for writers conferences. After the bios, the book is divided into three parts:

✓ Before a conference

✓ During a conference

✓ After a conference

In each section, your questions will be answered in articles on how to be prepared and how to put your best foot forward. Then we have provided links to the most helpful resources on the web. We hope you find this a fun and interactive research tool.

God created you for a purpose, and he gifted you with the ability to use words to inspire others and to shape culture. It is our prayer that as you read this book, you will find new tools that will alleviate the mystery of publishing and help you fulfill the dream you were called to.

If you'd like more information on the Northwest Christian Writers Association, you can find us on our webpage www.nwchristianwriters.org; our blog, http://nwchristianwriters.wordpress.com/; or look us up on LinkedIn groups, Facebook, and Twitter (@NWCWriters).

Five Successful People in the Writing Industry

James L. Rubart

Deciding You Are a Writer

by Dennis Brooke

One of the most popular novelists in the Christian market today once gave up his dream of becoming a writer. James L. Rubart, author of *Rooms* (B&H Publishing Group) and a string of other popular novels, had received what he felt was just one too many rejections. Even though he believed God called him to the craft, he set aside his first novel and gave up his dream. Then Darcie, his wife and number-one fan, told him, "At some point, you're going to have to decide you're a writer, whether anyone else believes in you or not." Jim listened, stepped out in faith, and achieved his dream.

Before he finally turned the publishing corner, Jim's primary career was as a marketing consultant. He is a popular speaker and noted expert on the subject of promoting yourself and your books. He's also the coauthor of *Novel Marketing,* scheduled for release in June 2013. You might expect a guru like Jim would credit his string of best-selling and award-winning books to the many promotion tactics he's learned during his marketing career. But—you'd be wrong. His primary recommendations for marketing your writing: work on the craft, create compelling ideas, and then *write* a great book. "For novelists, word of mouth is their biggest marketing tool," Jim says.

Focusing on the craft of writing and putting out great books has paid off for Jim. After publishing *Rooms, Book of Days,* and *The Chair* through B&H, this award-winning writer made the transition to being primarily a full-time author. He signed a five-book deal and published *Soul's Gate* with Thomas Nelson Publishers. His next Thomas Nelson novel, *Memory's Door* will be out in the summer of 2013. He now spends roughly 70 percent of his time writing, conducting interviews, and engaging in other writing-related activities.

> *You're going to have to decide you're a writer whether anyone else believes in you or not.*

Jim plans to build on the success of his novels by writing compelling short stories that he'll give away or sell cheaply via Amazon Kindle. He said, "As a novelist, this is a better use of my time than Facebook or Twitter." Jim hopes these short stories will build interest in his current novels and future releases.

Jim uses a unique system to organize his stories. He said, "I'm almost ADD when I write. I switch between scenes. I run from one idea to another. If you looked at my novel three weeks before I turned it in you wouldn't be able to follow it." He uses a decidedly low-tech method to organize his thoughts. "I need it big, bold, and large," he said. He starts by taking four sheets of paper and taping them together to sketch out scenes and ideas. This large sheet typically has a timeline, information about characters, and some of the major scenes. Then he jots down more detailed information about each scene on 3" x 5" index cards. Finally, he arranges everything on the window and walls of his writing room. This gives him a flexible organizational structure that he can rearrange as the story plays out. It eventually results in one of his compelling, supernatural novels.

Most of Jim's work is done in his hidden-away writing room accessible through a tiny door in the back of his son's closet. He settles into a black leather chair with his laptop—not at a desk. Surrounded by his oversized timeline sheet and scene index cards, he pounds away on the keys about three hours a day. Although for the first draft of his next novel, *Memory's Door,* he put in six-to-eight-hour spurts over five days.

How long does it take to get a first draft ready for an editor? *Rooms* took six years, although it was ten years before it was finally published. He turned out *Book of Days* in only two years, *The Chair* in five months, and *Soul's Gate* in ten weeks. *Memory's Door* took a mere six weeks.

His unique story lines are inspired from various sources. He said, "Lots of novelists have forty to fifty ideas on tap. I'm not like that. An idea pops into my brain, and I focus on that." His first novel, *Rooms*, was inspired by Robert Boyd Munger's booklet, *My Heart—Christ's Home* (InterVarsity Press). His father's struggle with Alzheimer's disease sparked the creation of *Book of Days*. The concept for *The Chair* came from a Chuck Colson article speculating that artifacts made by Jesus, the carpenter, might have lasted into the second century. Jim's first novel with Thomas Nelson, *Soul's Gate,* was the result of a brainstorming session with Allen Arnold, the former head of fiction at Thomas Nelson.

Jim is a big believer in the power of writers conferences to boost careers. But he encourages going to a conference with the right approach. "Too many writers go to a conference with the idea that if they don't walk away with contracts, they're failures. That puts tremendous pressure on beginning authors and robs them of the opportunity to learn and be inspired."

He likes to quote his friend Randy Ingermanson who says about conferences: "Don't think contracts—think contacts." Jim suggested that the best thing writers can do at a writers conference is to meet other authors and want-to-be authors. Jim said, "Learn from each other, and build relationships based on mutual belief and support." Instead of being "me" centered, he suggested, "Ask a person three questions before you say something about yourself. Trust that God is going to bring you the right meetings and the right relationships."

Jim is riding high as a popular writer who influences the world for Christ through intriguing stories, but that success almost eluded him. For years he struggled to finish his first book and to find an agent and publisher. He made a string of first-time author mistakes and faced many rejections. In fact, the low point came after being turned down by Allen Arnold, the same person who eventually became a great friend and helped him make the career change from marketing maven to author.

At one point, Jim believed his dream was dead. It was then Darci uttered those words of encouragement: "You're going to have to decide you're a writer whether anyone else believes in you or not." He took up the cause again, and his persistence finally paid off when B&H decided they would publish *Rooms*.

I had the pleasure of attending a church home group in Spokane that invited him to speak after *Rooms* was published. Person after person shared how Jim's freshman novel had inspired them and their friends. I was amazed how these people had been touched by a story that had been rejected by publisher after publisher. Fortunately, for those people and his many other fans, Jim didn't give up the fight. He trusted God and decided, "I *am* a writer."

* * *

Dennis Brooke *is a storyteller and aspiring novelist who tells stories at www.dennisbrooke.com He has written for international publications including* **Focus on the Family***,* **Toastmasters***, and* **Combat Crew magazines***.*

* * *

⊕ For Further Coaching:

All full links to author websites, articles and blog posts are provided at http://www.nwchristianwriters.org/

- ✓ To see James in his natural writing habitat, read Tricia Goyer's blog post *"My Writing Desk/James Rubart."*

- ✓ Director of Blue Ridge Mountains Christian Writers Conference and published novelist, Alton Gansky, interviews James on *Writer's Talk*.

- ✓ Jeff Gerke blogs at *Where the Map Ends: The Home of Christian Speculative Fiction*. When he's wearing a cape, he writes under the name Jefferson Scott. You can also learn more about this genre at *Marcher Lord Press*.

- ✓ Family Fiction is a source to find a list of Christian Speculative Fiction Authors.

- ✓ Tamara Lynn Kraft, on her blog *Word Sharpeners*, wrote a post on *"Speculative Genre,"* including a list of sub-categories for the genre.

- ✓ *"Author James Rubart Shares his Journey to Publication"* by Lynda Schab on the Christian Writing Examiner.

Marty Nystrom

Author and Songwriter

by Gigi Devine Murfitt

In the dead of night, Marty Nystrom quietly climbed to the fifteenth floor of a building in Mainland China. Accompanied by a group of people who smuggle Bibles into the underground church of China, Marty was there to lead worship. There was a quiet buzz in the apartment packed wall-to-wall with people.

The room erupted into loud praise and worship as Marty led them in song. It caught him off guard. He had expected the underground church to be subdued. But these people were hungry for God. He sang songs from a familiar Hosanna Music album and was blessed to learn they had been translated into their native tongue. The lyrics he had written had traveled across the world.

To avoid suspicion, the underground church never met twice in the same location. If anyone questioned the loud singing, the apartment owners told neighbors they were having a karaoke party. It was 1995, and karaoke was very popular in China.

Marty did not initially pursue song writing. It was a natural progression that came with each season of his life. When he taught school, he wrote music for his classes. He also composed songs to meet the needs of his church. Those songs eventually made their way beyond his local community and opened the door for a worldwide audience.

In 1981, Marty wrote one of my all-time favorite worship songs—*As the Deer*. There are over three hundred arrangements of this song on iTunes. It has been recorded by several Christian artists including Bryan Duncan, Phil Driscoll, and Chuck Girard.

The majority of the royalties Marty receives are from the performance, publishing, and recording of the songs he has written over the past three decades. He coauthored many of these songs, and in some cases, he provided only lyrics. Over one hundred of his songs were included on Integrity Music's worship and children's recordings.

When Marty was an elementary-school teacher, he noticed how students responded to the funny and quirky poems of Shel Silverstein. He believed that one day he would write a collection of poems that introduced nonchurched kids to the fascinating stories and characters in the Bible.

His dream became a reality in 2006 when Standard Publishing of Cincinnati, Ohio, released his children's book, *Don't Mess with Moses!: Peculiar Poems and Rib-*

Tickling Rhymes. He was thrilled when the publisher chose a well-known and established illustrator, *Steve Bjorkman.* This gave the book wider exposure, and he was very happy with the final product. His second book, *Zack, You're Acting Zany!: Playful Poems and Riveting Rhymes* came out in 2010.

Do not despise small beginnings

Marty was paid advances for both of his published books, which are recouped from future royalties. Once the advance is paid back, royalty checks begin.

Marty's helpful advice is useful for the writer of any genre.

1. Don't strive to figure out what to do in your writing career. Trust God for the timing of each project. Listen to the Holy Spirit for what God wants you to commit to writing. Marty shared several Scriptures to encourage writers in their journey.

   • "Humble yourselves, therefore, under God's mighty hand, that he may lift you up in due time" (1 Peter 5:6 NIV).

   • "Trust in the Lord with all your heart and lean not on your own understanding; in all your ways acknowledge him, and he will make your paths straight" (Proverbs 3:5–6).

   "But seek first his kingdom and his righteousness, and all these things will be given to you as well. Therefore do not worry about tomorrow, for tomorrow will worry about itself. Each day has enough trouble of its own" (Matthew 6:32–34).

2. Write engaging, relevant, and enjoyable words, aimed at the average reader. Try not to be preachy as you plant scriptural truths in the mind and heart of the reader. Aim for a message that will translate across cultural, denominational, and age groups.

3. Keep your desk and work area as sparse as possible. Marty keeps his resources and library in a separate room to remove any distraction from clutter or extra stimuli. He actually has two desks facing opposite walls with a swivel chair in between. One desk is dedicated to writing words and one to writing music.

4. Do not despise small beginnings. Begin writing in the arenas where you are known, such as newsletters or local church publications for your denomination.

5. Research and focus your submissions on the publishing houses that are looking for similar material. Refer to *The Christian Writer's Market Guide* by Jerry B. Jenkins and the Christian Writers' Guild.

6. Attend writers' events, and present work to publishers and agents. This is a great place to network and brainstorm with people in the publishing industry.

7. Solicit help to send out your manuscript submissions. Marty made it a summertime project for his junior-high son who sent out sample packets to publishers. He paid his son fifty cents for each packet he put together and mailed. Of the ninety-two submissions, he received three positive responses and chose to go with Standard Publishing. That's eighty-nine rejections! This approach may not work for all.

8. Be prepared to do your own publicity and marketing. Most publishers do not have a large publicity budget, and they expect authors to market their books. This aspect of publishing his books was a surprise to Marty.

9. Carve out time to write. With his busy lifestyle, Marty had to learn to write in the "nooks and crannies" of daily routine. His books were written during small chunks of time at Starbucks, airport layovers, and basketball game halftimes.

10. Toss out the good to focus on the best. Don't be an "idea hoarder" with an abundance of great plans but not enough follow-through. Learn to better catalogue ideas in order to access them when you need them.

11. Brainstorm away from your desk or workspace. Many of Marty's ideas come when he is walking, doing yard work, or driving his car. He has a handheld digital tape recorder that he takes everywhere he goes. Storing the ideas on this devise ensures they won't get lost.

12. Marty says, "I learned long ago that my right brain (creative side) functions best if I keep my left brain busy with a repetitious activity (walking, biking, etc.). When I just sit at my desk, my left brain

With his busy lifestyle, Marty had to learn to write in the "nooks and crannies" of daily routine

tends to interfere with thoughts like, 'I need to call so-and-so' or 'Did I turn the oven off?' or 'I should water that plant.' This also allows me to be open to the Holy Spirit—to breathe in his inspiration. Later, I type my ideas in an Excel spreadsheet and use its computing abilities to rank and categorize my ideas for better use."

13. Learn Microsoft Excel or another spreadsheet program to use as a tool for organizing your work. A spreadsheet is typically thought of as a tool for processing numbers, but it has many features that work great for the wordsmith. With it you can organize and search for ideas. You can also build lists and databases to use as references for your writing. (Examples: list of colors, adjectives, names, etc. you would like to use in future manuscripts.)

Marty enjoys writing short pieces that provide a feeling of completion and satisfaction along the way. When asked about writing a novel, he said, "The thought of writing a full novel is daunting. I have great admiration for those who write longer works."

Marty's highly recommended published works can be purchased online at the major bookstores. His music is available on iTunes. (Links included above)

✻ ✻ ✻

Gigi Devine Murfitt *writes and speaks about God's work in her life. She is the author of* **Caregiver's Devotions to Go (See Media, 2010)** *and coauthor of* **My Message is C.L.E.A.R. (Gabriel's Foundation of Hope, 2012)**. *She is a member of the Northwest Christian Writers Association and The Speaker's Connection.*

✻ ✻ ✻

🕐 **For Further Coaching:**

All full links to author websites, articles and blog posts are provided at http://www.nwchristianwriters.org/

- ✓ During his poetry workshop at the 2010 Northwest Christian Writers Renewal, Marty Nystrom recommended two websites for poetry writing, *Rhyme Zone* and *OneLook Dictionary Search*.

- ✓ On the Christian Copyright Licensing International site, Marty teaches the "*10 Traits the Top CCLI Songs have in Common.*"

- ✓ Modern hymn writers, Keith and Kristyn Getty, were interviewed by Stan Guthrie in a post called "*Singable Doctrine*" for Christianity Today.

✓ Fernando Ortega's workshop from the *National Worship Leader Conference* was reviewed in the article, *"Songwriting Tips from Fernando Ortega"* on the blog, *Worship Matters: Resources for Music, Worship, & More* from Bob Kauflin.

Marcus Yoars

Through the Eyes of an Editor

By Kim Martinez

He pushes through the double doors, arms laden with sample magazines, and pauses for a moment to take in the vibrant energy of yet another writers conference. While many attend conferences to learn and grow, the role of an editor is different. The editor attends to discover.

Recently, I had the opportunity to connect with *Marcus Yoars* of *Charisma magazine.* I first met Marcus at an editor appointment at the Northwest Christian Writers Conference in 2012. Marcus looks like he played football, presents with the intensity of a youth pastor, and relates with a relaxed, easygoing style. I was so impressed with him that I reorganized my workshop choices to make sure I garnered as much wisdom as possible.

The opportunity to interview Marcus was a real treat. What writer wouldn't take time to learn what goes on in the mind of an editor?

The one thing that came through in my conversation with Marcus was the picture I started above: Marcus, laden with extra copies of *Charisma* magazines, pushing his way through the doors of a conference with a sense of intrigue. Who will he meet at *this* conference? Which writer will understand his audience and be just the right personality to provide intriguing, consistent content? Somewhere in this crowd, someone is ready to join the *Charisma* writing team. Who will it be, and will Marcus be able to find him or her before the conference ends?

Marcus didn't start out to be an editor. A missionary kid raised in Hong Kong, Marcus studied journalism and English at an Alabama college where football was king. If writing was his first love, music wasn't far behind. In fact, in high school Marcus thought he'd be a sports writer who led worship and wrote music on the side.

Immediately following college, Marcus served as worship pastor for a small church. He entered the publishing world with a job at Thomas Nelson Bibles, then worked as a managing editor for various magazines at LifeWay. Yet music continued to call him, and he quit the nine-to-five world to travel full time with a Christian band. To pay the bills, Marcus reached out to his publishing industry contacts for freelance work.

If you haven't discovered it yet, the publishing industry

> *It isn't enough to have good ideas; good writers know how to connect those ideas to the best (and often largest) audience possible*

has a lot to do with relationships. From his time as an editor, Marcus had developed relationships with other editors and writers. Those contacts brought him steady writing gigs, which made the transition easier when he eventually left the music scene and returned to full-time editorial work. He worked as a ghostwriter or editor with several major Christian authors, including Benny Hinn, T. D. Jakes, Stephen Arterburn, Max Lucado, John MacArthur, and Dutch Sheets.

His writing relationship with Dutch Sheets led to connections at Charisma Media. Today Marcus is not only the editor of *Charisma* magazine but is also the editorial director for Charisma Media's Content Development department, which produces multiple magazines, websites, newsletters, apps, and other digital media.

As you can see, connections, relationships, reliability, and consistency are important aspects of Marcus' career. They are also some of the things he is looking for in writers when he attends writers conferences.

Not one to be stuck behind a computer screen, Marcus feels that "there is nothing like getting out and connecting with people live." Social media has changed the dynamics, but Marcus enjoys keeping those people connections—keeping it real.

Imagine a Tuesday morning. Marcus hits the office, and several deadlines loom. He meets with his editorial staff, each of whom is in charge of a different publication or website with different audiences. Yet Marcus is in charge of pulling them all together under the Charisma brand.

When Marcus returns from a writers conference, he hopes to have contact information for quality writers who can truly connect with Charisma's various audiences through their writing. You need to know two things in order to make it to Marcus' go-to list of freelance writers:

1. **Come with solid pitches.** Think through why you are pitching to this editor. Know the editor's audience, and match your pitch to the publication. The editor would rather not have to guess why or how your story idea will resonate with the magazine's audience. Every magazine has a different approach on this, but it's your job to figure out the approach of the publication and direct your pitch accordingly.

   It's all about connections. Content is king, but the whole point of the content is to connect with people

2. **Think like a marketer.** Don't think like the annoying multilevel guy who won't take no for an answer. Instead, think like the savvy Fifth Avenue marketing pro who knows what his client had for breakfast, why he had it, and why he needs this product to make tomorrow's breakfast better. Writers must know their audiences. That's always

been the case. But in today's environment, they must also know how to market their ideas to those audiences. It isn't enough to have good ideas; good writers know how to connect those ideas to the best (and often largest) audience possible. Today's editors look for marketing-savvy writers who can extend their influence—and message— beyond just the copy they turn in.

As an editor, Marcus' job is to provide great content that his readers need and rely on. To do that, he relies on writers who prove they are consistent and reliable. Most editors today must create exponentially more content than in years past, all with reduced in-house staffs. This makes for a busy, pressure-filled office in which editors are constantly seeking freelance writers whom they know will deliver what they need when they need it.

Back to the beginning scene. As Marcus drops his sample magazines down on the resource table, his hostess hands him a water bottle and shows him to the room for his editor/agent appointments.

He takes a moment to stretch his tall frame, turns toward the windows, and prays over the hours ahead. He will get the opportunity to introduce his brand and serve the audience of writers, but most of all, Marcus wants to find some "God connections."

In Marcus' words, "It's all about connections. Content is king, but the whole point of the content is to connect with people."

* * *

Kim Martinez *is an ordained Assemblies of God pastor with a master's of theology degree from Fuller Seminary. She is a ministry and life-development coach and can be found online at* www.deepimprints.com *and* www.getunstuckbootcamp.com. *She writes a weekly column for* **ministrytodaymag.com**.

* * *

For Further Coaching:

All full links to author websites, articles and blog posts are provided at http://www.nwchristianwriters.org/

- ✓ For spiritual encouragement, Marcus offers *"Twenty-six Words That Can Change Your Life"* on LifeWay.

- ✓ Writers Conference Guidelines printed a post, *"Meeting with Faculty: Be Prepared and Professional."*

- ✓ *"The Scoop on the Dreaded Fifteen Minute Appointment"* by Edie Melsom creator of the blog, *The Write Conversation*.

- ✓ Nick Harrison, Senior Editor at *Harvest House Publishers* blogged about *"Writing Mistakes."*

Robin Jones Gunn
Surprised by God's Plans

By Mindy Peltier

Robin Jones Gunn didn't dream of being a writer, she dreamed of being a missionary. At the age of twelve at Bible camp, she committed her life to overseas missions and pursued this ambition through adulthood.

People often identified her as a natural storyteller and urged her to write, but she felt confident of her missionary calling.

In 1976, at the college missions' conference, *Urbana*, she filled out a survey to determine her suitability for an overseas mission assignment. She was surprised to see that she was matched up with an opening to be a laundry supervisor in Nairobi, Africa. Robin said, "It wasn't exactly what I had in mind, but I applied anyway." She was willing to wash clothes if she could tell the African people about God's love.

Her application was rejected. Brokenhearted that she wasn't even qualified to do the laundry, she shared her experience with her girls' Sunday school class. One student timidly raised her hand and said, "Maybe you should tell stories instead."

Robin still didn't feel called to write.

She married a youth pastor, and they started a family. Recognizing her abilities, her husband strongly urged her to attend a writers conference in 1980. Robin went and heeded the call to write. The gift others recognized soon bore fruit in published articles, devotions, and interviews. By 1982 Robin's first children's books were published.

When Robin challenged the teen girls in their youth group about the books they were reading, they asked her to write ones they could read. The *Christy Miller series* was born, followed by the *Sierra Jensen* and *Katie Weldon* series.

To fit writing into a life blessed with a husband, two kids, ministry, and hospitality, Robin wrote from 3:00 a.m. until 7:30 a.m. three days a week. She continued this for years and still uses this schedule on occasion to meet deadlines.

Robin loves writers conferences because they provide opportunities to meet with writers, editors, publishers, and agents in one place. She passes on this encouragement to first-time attendees: "Don't be afraid. We were all in that same place

Be prepared to be surprised by God. He has planted these dreams in your heart

at one time. See yourself as a professional. Believe that God has opened the door for you to attend this conference for a reason, and remind yourself that you don't want insecurities to get in the way of discovering that reason."

Robin encourages going to a conference prepared. "Come with business cards and a winsome, succinct, articulate answer to the question, 'What are you working on?' You will repeat this answer dozens of times, so practice before you go. It will be the same answer to similar questions such as, 'What have you published?' and 'What sort of writing interests you?' and 'What brought you to the conference?' Be ready to promote yourself and your writing interests without hesitancy. Own it."

A writers conference is usually the only time you are able to approach editors or agents, so Robin understands the fear most writers have. "Don't overdo your pitch, and don't throw yourself under to the bus. Just state the truth. You obviously have a passion for what you're working on or else you wouldn't be at the conference. I've listened to hundreds—maybe thousands—of pitches from beginning writers over the years. The ones that grab my attention are those where writers look me in the eye and clearly articulate the basics of their writing projects without apology or arrogance. I've only experienced that sort of professional pitch a dozen or so times. Those are the ones that get noticed."

She also encourages writers to be in frequent contact with other writers. "'Iron sharpens iron.' God's Word tells us that. I would be so dull without the ongoing fellowship with other writers."

Robin believes writers' relationships are necessary for more than fellowship. She encourages writers to find a monthly gathering with other writers and a small critique group to hone their skills.

"Writers need to seek out those circles of kindred spirits in order to go the distance in this industry. Many of the most strategic steps in my long career as a writer happened as a result of input from other writers, editors, publishers, and agents. If I would have convinced myself that it cost too much or was too much effort to get out the door and go to a workshop, conference, or critique group, I know that I would have been thwarted at many crossroads," said Robin.

She acknowledges her success was influenced by these relationships. "I know certain books would never have been written or published if I didn't make the effort and pay the price in time and money to network with others in the publishing world."

To date, Robin has written eighty-five books that have been translated into nine different languages. Her recent friendship fiction series *Sisterchicks* for adult women has won several awards. She has written many nonfiction works as well.

What about her early dream of bringing the love of Jesus overseas? Her faithful desire was answered in the Lord's way. Robin met an African woman at a LittWorld Conference who was encouraged by Robin's books. When Robin shared her tale of rejection as a laundry supervisor, the African sister said, "You didn't need to come to Nairobi to wash our clothes. God sent your books and they washed our hearts."

Robin recognized the hand of the Lord. "I didn't go to Africa but those stories did."

Her advice to writers is: "Be prepared to be surprised by God. He has planted these dreams in your heart. If it's fire in the belly, it won't go away. But maybe you are restricting the way those dreams can go by placing limits on how it has to happen. Open your heart."

Then let the Lord fill your open heart with his plans, as he did for Robin.

✳ ✳ ✳

Mindy Peltier *has blogged over a thousand posts about her life as a Christian homeschooling mom, grandma, thyroid-cancer patient, and writer at In* **the Write Moment**. *She serves on the board of directors for the Northwest Christian Writers Association and is a member of the Oregon Christian Writers. You will find Mindy online at* www.mommamindy. wordpress.com

✳ ✳ ✳

For Further Coaching:

All full links to author websites, articles and blog posts are provided at http://www.nwchristianwriters.org/

✓ Read why *Jeffrey Zaslow*, columnist for *the Wall Street Journal*, interviewed Robin Jones Gunn in *"An Unusual Request for an Interview"* posted on her blog.

✓ *How to Write a Novel: The Snowflake Method"* by Randy Ingermanson, self-proclaimed Mad Professor of Fiction Writing, teaching online at *Advanced Fiction Writing.*

✓ *"Truth in Fiction"* by Kaye Dacus on her site Kay Dacus: Humor, Hope, and Happily Ever Afters.

✓ *"Breathing Life into Your Fiction Writing by Author Janalyn Voigt"* on Gina Holmes's website *Novel Rocket: Getting Your Book off the Ground.*

✓ Ellie Whyte's website *Soul Inspirationz* for Quality Christian Fiction posted *"Featured Author Interview with Tracie Peterson."*

✓ Celebrate National Novel Writing Month, NaNoWriMo, by writing a 50,000 word novel from November 1–30.

✓ *"102 Resources for Fiction Writing"* listed on the blog, Here to Create.

✓ On *The Moral Premise Blog: Story Structure Craft* Stanley D. Williams published, *"How is the Moral Premise Evident in Every Scene?"* His visual, *The Story Diamond Key* is on his website *The Moral Premise: Harnessing Virtue and Vice for Box Office Success.*

A Literary Agent's Perspective on Conferences

by Lesley Ann McDaniel

What would it take for a farm boy from Canada to become one of the most highly regarded literary agents in Christian publishing? For Les Stobbe, founder of *Leslie H. Stobbe Literary Agency*, it took God playing connect-the-dots with an abundance of rich life experiences.

A career spanning fifty-four years as writer, editor, and agent had its unlikely beginning with a mountain climbing accident that resulted in a four-month hospital stay. It was during this time that Les spotted an ad in *Christian Life* magazine with the heading, "You Can Write." He paid $15 for the seven-lesson course, and his career was off and running.

With a degree in pastoral theology and two years of article-writing experience to his credit, Les became the founding editor of the *Mennonite Observer*, compiling twelve pages of news and inspiration every week without the benefit of an assistant.

After four years, he took a year off to teach at a Christian high school. Before that year was out, he was hired by Moody Press to supervise the selling floor of their bookstore. Within six months, he was spending half days as manuscript-evaluation editor for Kenneth Taylor at Moody Press.

This eventually led to a job as editor of *Christian Bookseller* magazine (later became *Christian Retailing)* and associate editor of *Christian Life* magazine, then four years as business-magazine editor in his native Canada. Moody Press called again, and he led their editorial team for eight years, serving as sole acquisitions editor for a list of one hundred or more books, including the *Ryrie Study Bible*. He then became vice president for books and book clubs at *Christian Herald* in Chappaqua, New York. Living in Danbury, Connecticut, he and his wife helped found what became the Walnut Hill Community Church.

Preparing to be a writer is a marathon, not a sprint

Eventually, financial losses at the *Christian Herald* magazine became God's way of moving Les to San Bernardino, California. After eleven years as editorial director then as president of Here's Life Publishers, he oversaw the company being sold to Thomas Nelson Publishers.

At this point in his career, several writer friends approached him at a conference and asked him to represent them. For the next eleven years, he worked part-time as literary agent while acting as managing editor of the curriculum division of Scripture Press. The sale of Scripture Press led him to a position as vice president of communications and marketing at the Evangelistic Association of New England.

Five years later, the dot-com bust shut down so much foundation giving that he was released to be engaged by Jerry B. Jenkins to write a curriculum for the newly acquired *Christian Writers' Guild*. After a year as Journalist in Residence at Gordon College and teaching journalism courses, he retired to become a full-time literary agent.

Les attends up to ten writers conferences a year, where he meets many of the writers he mentors and represents. Here are some of his *insights* for writers planning to attend a conference:

What are you looking for as an agent when you attend a writers conference?

> *My overarching goal is to help writers succeed, so I do a lot of mentoring. But then I also look for book projects that have publishing possibilities. In today's publishing environment, I am looking for nonfiction with what I call "added value," something really special beyond a straight manuscript. In fiction, I'm looking for writers who have studied the most popular genres and have written for the market that's out there.*

For a writer, what, in your opinion, are the benefits of attending a conference?

> *The absolutely number-one benefit is meeting editors and agents who provide perspective and opportunity.*

The second most important benefit is honing your craft through gaining as much as possible through continuing classes and workshops. One best-selling writer went to thirteen conferences before he wrote his first novel, but he also read constantly. Another writer with forty books confessed she attended five conferences before she felt she really had the information needed to be successful. Preparing to be a writer is a marathon, not a sprint.

Considering the current publishing climate, are conferences more or less beneficial than they have been in past years?

Years ago there might have been two conferences attracting editors. Now there are many large conferences attracting editors and agents. That makes them more beneficial. We also have more skilled writers leading continuing classes and workshops.

Are you ever surprised by what catches your interest during a pitch session?

Absolutely. Like a book on the Daniel fast in which the author had photographed one hundred dishes; a writer who had teamed up with a super sonographic operator to show me pictures of a baby's development in the womb; a writer who had a one-on-one discipleship manual with text in multiple colors and had endorsements by really big- name authors.

What would you say is the most common mistake made by writers pitching to you?

Coming across as super confident and bordering on arrogance turns me off every time. Humility goes a long way. It's what is written for readers that counts, not the author's super hype.

What is your number one tip for a writer to get the most out of a conference?

When approaching editors or agents, come prepared with a three-minute pitch, and then quietly let them read either a synopsis or into the first chapter. Answer questions quietly and humbly.

The path God set for Les equipped him with the skills needed for his role as a literary agent, which he has served in for the past seventeen years. He is also executive editor of the *Jerry B. Jenkins Christian Writers Guild*, and the director of International Christian Writers. He has written fourteen books and hundreds of published articles. He and Rita, his wife of fifty-six years, have two children and five grandchildren.

Visit Les Stobbe's website at www.stobbeliterary.com.

* * *

Lesley Ann McDaniel *juggles a career in theatrical costuming with writing women's and young adult fiction. She has completed four novels and is a member of Northwest Christian Writers Association, American Christian Fiction Writers, and an amazing critique group. She enjoys living under the blue skies of Seattle with her husband and two kids. In her spare time, she chips away at her goal of reading every book ever written. Visit her at www.lesleyannmcdaniel.com.*

* * *

🕐 **For Further Coaching:**

All full links to author websites, articles and blog posts are provided at http://www.nwchristianwriters.org/

- ✓ On his website for the Leslie H. Stobbe Literary Agency, Les Stobbe clearly defines "*The Role of a Literary Agent.*"

- ✓ American Christian Fiction Writer (ACFW) writer Rachel Wilder blogged on Les Stobbe's ACFW conference workshop *Fiction Writing: Passion, Calling, Ministry, or Business?*, giving his insight on fiction writing.

- ✓ "Literary Agent Les Stobbe Discusses Ways Authors Can Increase Book Sales" featured on *The Barn Door*.

- ✓ Rachelle Gardner, of Books & Such Literary Agency, blogged "*How Do You Find a Literary Agent?*"

- ✓ Michael Hyatt Intentional Leadership wrote "*Before You Hire a Literary Agent*" and "*Literary Agents Who Represent Christian Authors.*"

- ✓ Jeff Gerke advises on "*Understanding Agents*" in his blog, *Where the Map Ends*.

- ✓ "*Juggling Agent Interest*" by Tamela Hancock Murray of The Steve Laube Agency.

- ✓ Fiction Writer's Connection wrote "*Firing Your Agent.*"

- ✓ www.Barndoorbookloft.net Literary Agent Les Stobbe discusses ways authors can increase book sales. April 27, 2011 Issue

A Beginning Writer's Prayer

By Lydia E. Harris

Dear Lord,

I sense you're nudging me to write. I've resisted, made excuses: "I can't write. I don't have anything to say. No one will read my writing." Now it's a matter of obedience. If you ask me to write, I will.[1]

Where do I begin? How do I get organized? Please bring mentors, encouragers, and others further along the writing path to help me.

This new writing field seems like a vast ocean of information. I'm cautious, sticking in my big toe, testing the water. Brrr! It's cold, overwhelming. I'm not sure I want to plunge in. I may get soaked, even drown. Please keep me afloat with your reassurance and guidance.[2] Apart from you I can do nothing.[3]

Life experiences swirl in my head. Which ideas would help others? I don't want my writing to be useless.

I'm concerned about my motives. Are they pure? Am I writing in obedience to help others or for recognition?

Lord, purify my heart and motives.[4] Let my writing glorify you alone. If success comes, help me give you the credit.[5] If rejection comes, remind me my worth is based on your thoughts of me, not what editors and publishers think. You love and accept me whether or not a word is ever printed.[6] I'll work for your "well done, good and faithful servant."[7]

Please keep my life in balance and my writing in perspective. Help me discern your voice[8] from the enemy's discouraging voice.

This is a new adventure, Lord. The best part is you and me—working together—to accomplish your purpose through my life.[9] Give me the strength and courage to plunge in and keep swimming.[10] I'm confident you'll complete the work you have begun in me[11] because he who calls us is faithful.[12] I thank you, in the name of Jesus, the author and finisher of my faith.[13] Amen.

This prayer is based on the following NIV scriptures.

1. Jeremiah 7:23

2. Isaiah 48:17–18

3. John 15:5

4. Psalm 51:10

5. Psalm115:1

6. Jeremiah 31:3

7. Matthew 25:21

8. John 10:27

9. Psalms 138:8

10. Joshua 1:9

11. Philippians 1:6

12. 1 Thessalonians 5:24

13. Hebrews 12:2

Before a
Writers
Conference

Seven Tips to Get the Most from Writers Conferences

By Melissa K. Norris

Read any agents' or editors' blogs, and you'll most likely find them advising you to attend at least one writers conference a year. There are many to choose from; location and price will influence your choice.

So you've done it. You've paid your fee, reserved your hotel room, and are ready to be inspired and attend the conference. Whether you're a newbie or a veteran attendee, you can always make your experience better.

Pack Wisely

You want to portray yourself as a professional, but conferences make for long days. Business casual is a good option, and it's better to err on the side of overdressing rather than underdressing. You'd rather be seen as professional, not sloppy. Choose low-heeled shoes or flats. No tennis shoes. Dress in layers. Some rooms are hot, others cold.

Come Prepared

Bring a large purse or small tote. Most rooms have water glasses, but bring a water bottle along just in case. Bring a small snack, granola bar, or banana if you get hungry in between meals. Bring a notebook for taking notes and storing handouts from classes. If you have them, bring copies of your synopsis, proposal, and manuscript. Never hand them to agents or editors unless asked first. Most prefer to not take hard copies. Can you imagine flying home with all that paper? But I have had an agent request my hard copy, and I was glad I had it available at the conference.

Hone Your Pitch

If you're meeting with an agent or editor, have your pitch worked out ahead of time. Write it down on a notecard. Be conscientious of the others' time in group appointments. No one, including the agent/editor, likes a time hog.

Consider business cards

You can print them yourself or go to sites like www.vistaprint.com for inexpensive cards. Include your name, e-mail, website, blog, social media links, and what you write.

Be social

This is your chance to surround yourself with other writers, people who understand you and what you do. Even if you

Chitchat with people who get you and this crazy calling of being a writer

don't know anyone there, find people sitting or standing alone and ask them what they write. (Remember to return the favor if asked.) I met my business partner, the owner of the literary agency I'm represented by, and was hired to speak at another writers conference, all from contacts I made at writers conferences.

Pray

Really. Ask God to lead you to people at the conference. Dedicate yourself to asking him for direction in your writing career. I promise he will show you the way to the path he wants for you. Spend time before, during, and after the conference in prayer. Pray for those you met and connected with as well, not just your own future.

Relax

You are taking a step forward in your writing career. You are honing your craft. Enjoy this time focusing on your gift. Chitchat with people who get you and this crazy calling of being a writer. When you say story arc, they'll know what you're talking about. Query letter, platform—all those terms the rest of the world doesn't understand. You're among your people at a writers conference. Live it up!

* * *

Melissa K. Norris *is a novelist, newspaper columnist, and author of* **Pioneering Today: Faith and Home the Old-Fashioned Way**. *Visit her website to inspire your faith and pioneer roots.* http://www.melissaknorris.com *She is also co-owner of TriLink, a social media mentoring company.* http://www.trilink-social-media.com

* * *

🕐 For Further Coaching:

All full links to author websites, articles and blog posts are provided at http://www.nwchristianwriters.org/

- ✓ Edie Melson from *The Write Conversation,* gives readers the *"Top 10 Reasons to Attend a Writers Conference."*

- ✓ Sandra Bishop from the MacGregor Literary Agency wrote about *"Pat the Conferee"* for the Northwest Christian Writers Association blog.

- ✓ Jan Cline, founder and director of the Inland Northwest Christian Writers Conference, offers *"Three Survival Tips for Conference Goers."*

- ✓ The question, *"Are Writers Conferences a Worthwhile Investment?"* was answered by Chip MacGregor of MacGregor Literary Agency.

- ✓ W. Terry Whalin, on his site *Right-Writing.com,* tells *"Why a Writer's Conference is Important."*

- ✓ *"Writers' Conference Advice"* by Ginnie Wiehardt on *About.com Fiction Writing*

- ✓ To find writers' events in your area, Shaw Guides lists *Guide to Writers Conferences & Writing Workshops.*

- ✓ James Scott Bell, as a guest blogger for the Steve Laube Agency, commands *"Get Thee to a Writers Conference."*

Conquering Conference Jitters

by Lydia E. Harris

The writers conference was almost over, and I still hadn't met with any editors, publishers, or agents. I had preregistered for several appointments, so why weren't any scheduled? When I inquired, I learned the appointments were posted on the wall. I checked and found my name in several places. Aghast, I realized I had missed them all! But they weren't with the editors I had requested anyway.

Then I awoke from my dream. (Perhaps it was more of a nightmare.) Let me reassure you, this is not what happens at conferences.

This preconference dream alerted me to my anxiety about an upcoming conference only a week away. Although I had attended numerous conferences and even taught at many, I still experienced preconference jitters. I know I'm not alone. So what's a writer to do?

I e-mailed several people for prayer support. Jan, a fellow writer, replied, "Most of all, go to have fun."

Go for Fun

Have fun? What a novel concept! No one had ever suggested that before. I felt stressed because I had focused on preparing my writing just right and shopping for clothes to look just right to make the just right first impression. And, of course, I needed to select the right workshops and classes and request appointments with the right editors, publishers, and agents. These were all important, but I had exaggerated them in my mind.

Besides, I wanted to get my money's worth from the conference and hoped to sell some writing to help pay for it. Would any editors be interested in my manuscripts?

Whew! I was putting lots of pressure on myself. Many high expectations were riding on that conference. No wonder I had a bad dream. As I prepared, the thought of fun was not on my list.

Jan's advice changed my focus, and I e-mailed her, "Fun, I can handle. Maybe I should bring a red hat."

"And wear it with orange," she replied.

But if you go to meet with God, he'll meet you where you are and make all the right connections for you

I didn't own a red hat, but I packed my frivolous red shawl with the fuzzy fringe and headed for the conference. I wore it and had fun. And God made all the right connections for me.

Don't let jitters like mine keep you from attending a conference. Instead, use these tips to conquer them.

Jitter-Busting Tips

1. Admit your jitters and share them.

2. Realize you're not alone.

3. Bring your anxieties to God in prayer, and ask him to guide your preparations.

4. Enlist prayer support from others: family, friends, your church, and fellow writers.

5. Encourage a good friend to attend the conference with you for moral support.

6. Seek advice from veteran conferees on classes and workshops to attend.

7. Do your homework on editors and agents so you feel prepared to meet with them instead of worrying.

8. Prepare manuscripts that meet the needs of publications that interest you.

9. Take clothing you feel comfortable in and items that look good on you.

10. Focus on others, not just yourself. Ask God to use you in the lives of other conferees.

11. Take a teachable spirit, and go with open expectations.

12. Realize the conference won't be perfect. Plan to have fun and enjoy it anyway.

One final tip: If you expect to meet the right editor who will buy the right manuscript, you may be disappointed. But if you go to meet with God, he'll meet you where you are and make all the right connections for you.

So armed with these tips to conquer jitters, I hope to meet you at the next conference.

* * *

Lydia E. Harris, *MA in Home Economics, has attended numerous writers conferences and teaches at them. She has accumulated hundreds of bylines, contributed to 17 books, and writes a bimonthly column titled* **"A Cup of Tea with Lydia."** *Her five grandkids call her "Grandma Tea," and together they develop and test recipes that are published in* **Focus on the Family** *magazines. Lydia wrote the practical and inspiring Bible study,* **Preparing My Heart for Grandparenting**.

* * *

🕐**For Further Coaching:**

All full links to author websites, articles and blog posts are provided at http://www.nwchristianwriters.org/

- ✓ *"How God Can Use Your Anxiety for Good"* by Laura Ortberg Turner on the blog *Her.menuetics: Christian Women*. Cultural Comment. by *Christianity Today*.

✓ Julia Bettencourt posted her devotional *"Keep Calm"* on her site, *Creative Ladies Ministry*.

✓ Mount Hermon Christian Writers Conference offers testimonies of writers who have been blessed by their conference experience.

Be Prepared!
How to Make a Conference Binder

By Janalyn Voigt

While the conference you attend will probably provide you with a folder, you can look more professional if you carry a binder you've organized ahead of time. It's also a great help, making sure you'll find what you need when you need it while at the conference. Start with an attractive, low-key binder. Using page protectors, dividers, and pockets, depending on your preference, add the following:

Front Matter

In the front of your binder, include three-or-four page protectors for travel specifications (like flight details or driving directions), a schedule you print in advance from the conference site with tentative class selections marked, and information on your pitch sessions.

Business Cards

Whether or not you give your business cards to agents and editors, you'll probably want to give them to other writers at the conference. Your business card should feature your name and any contact information you're willing to provide. At the minimum, include your e-mail address. Be sure to list any website or blog you may have. You can also include a Twitter handle or other social networking address if it's where you most often can be found. If you want the option of writing on the back, leave it blank and unfinished. A quick Internet search will turn up sites that offer business cards. Many of them will allow you to design business cards inexpensively online. It's also possible to work through a printer in your area.

One Sheets

Presented in a pleasing graphic design, a one sheet is an optional sell sheet that typically features an image or logo to represent your story, a plot summary, and a few enticing details about the project. That will highlight marketing aspects, why you are specially qualified to write it, your biography, an author image, and contact information. If you have Microsoft Word, you will find templates in the left sidebar of the page that opens when you select "New" from the main menu. The nice thing about having a one sheet for your project

A conference binder can help you feel prepared and at your best, lending you confidence at a time when you need it most

is that agents or editors may be willing to take it, whereas they may not want to accept a bulky proposal due to airline weight restrictions.

Sample Chapters

Print three or four copies of your manuscript, and secure them with small binder clips rather than staples. You may not need these, but it's better to have them on hand in case editors or agents want to take them. Some people copy their proposals and sample chapters on a CD to offer as take-homes at pitch sessions. This can sometimes be successful.

Proposal(s)

Print several copies of the proposal for each book-length project you plan to pitch. Don't be surprised if these remain in your binder. Like sample chapters, it's better to have them on hand in case you need them.

Tear Sheets or Photocopies

If you intend to pitch articles, have either tear sheets or good-quality photocopies of your published articles on hand.

Biographies

At the minimum, study and print out the information provided by the conference on the editors and agents you hope to see. Visit their websites, and include any relevant information (like their submission guidelines) in a special section of your binder. Consult these to refresh your memory just prior to your pitch session.

Thank-You Cards

It's good form but hard to find the time after the conference to send thank-you cards to those who benefited you. If you place return-address stickers and stamps on your cards ahead of time, all you have to do is fill in the recipient's name with a brief message, then address, and mail them right from the conference.

Phone Numbers of Your Contacts

Prior to leaving for the conference, make sure you have up-to-date phone numbers for those you would like to meet and/or spend time with. It's fun to schedule a few lunches and meetings, but leave room for spontaneity as well.

Pens, Pencils, Highlighters

Using a three-ring pencil pocket will prevent you from fishing in your purse or pocket for writing implements.

A conference binder can help you feel prepared and at your best, lending you confidence at a time when you need it most.

* * *

Janalyn Voigt *is a novelist, literary judge, and avid reader. She serves as a writing mentor through her* **Live Write Breathe** *site and as a social media mentor via* **TriLink Social Media Mentors**. *Her epic fantasy series,* **Tales of Faeraven**, *begins with* **DawnSinger**. *She also writes historical fiction and is represented by* **Wordserve Literary**.

* * *

⏱ **For Further Coaching:**

All full links to author websites, articles and blog posts are provided at http://www.nwchristianwriters.org/

- ✓ "*What to Wear at a Writers Conference*" by Edie Melson from *The Write Conversation*.

- ✓ Karen Evans advises "*What to Bring to a Writers Conference*" at Extras for Authors.

- ✓ Writermorphosis: The Process of Becoming, and Remaining, a Writer posted the "*Writers Conference Tool Kit: What to Bring.*"

- ✓ "*Creating an Author Press Kit*" by Debbie Ridpath Ohi on *Writing World*.

Create a Compelling Book Proposal

by Lynnette Bonner

A proposal is a concise document authors use to entice publishers into taking a second look at their manuscripts. Most major publishers have specific proposal guidelines on their website. This article will give a general overview of content most publishers expect to see in a proposal. Each paragraph below should be a section in your proposal.

Title Page

The title of your manuscript should be centered a third of the way down the page with the author's name in a smaller font just below it. "A Proposal" should also be clearly visible on this page. Resist the urge to go fancy! Keep fonts clean and legible.

Table of Contents

If editors want to skip to a certain section, they should be able to quickly find which page to go to.

Book Summary

It is often good to give three overviews of varying length, one of approximately thirty words, one of about one hundred fifty words, and one of about three hundred words. Each one should build on the last and give a stronger and more compelling reason for the editor to keep reading. Various people at the publishing house will use these to inform (and hopefully entice) others of the book's contents.

Target Market

Identify the audience for your book, and state any pertinent information about that market the publisher may need to know in order to make an informed decision.

Character Description (fiction only)

Give a short paragraph description of each main character in your story.

Chapter Synopsis

Give a synopsis of each chapter in your book. The completed synopsis should be one to four pages at most.

For nonfiction, give short chapter descriptions. Emphasize the benefits for readers—what they will get out of each chapter.

Author Bio

A proposal should contain a catchy but short author biography. Tell what qualifies you to write this story or nonfiction book. List your important published books or articles.

Marketing Plan

Give some information about your platform and publicity reach, such as the number of blog followers, Facebook fans and friends,

Add any concrete plans you intend to put into effect for marketing the story

and Twitter followers. Also include any professional organizations you belong to that might help you with publicity or marketing. Add any concrete plans you intend to put into effect for marketing the story.

Competitive Works

List books that are similar to yours. Check out Amazon, Fiction Finder, or your local library to find information about published books that are similar to the one you are proposing. Give the titles, genres, and authors' names. If you can find sales data, include that in this section. Tell why your book is similar and also what will make your book a different.

Deliverables

Include information on how much of the book you currently have completed, when you think you can finish and deliver it, and any other special features you envision or can provide for your book.

If you have secured endorsements from other authors or celebrities, make sure to include a section for them.

First Three Chapters

Polished and ready to go!

The entire proposal should have a header or footer with the proposal title, author's last name, and a page number in it. (Don't put this on the title page of the proposal.)

Once you have each section written out, put the proposal together in a plain two- pocket style folder with your business card in the slot on the left and the proposal neatly inserted in the right-hand pocket so that the title and your name are on top.

For an example of a fiction proposal, see my website at the following link: www.lynnettebonner/ficproposalsample.com.

* * *

Lynnette Bonner's *current releases include the four books in* **The Shepherd's Heart series**, **Rocky Mountain Oasis**, **High Desert Haven**, **Fair Valley Refuge**, **Spring Meadow Sanctuary**, *and her newest romantic suspense release,* **The Unrelenting Tide**. *Lynnette makes her home in the beautiful Pacific Northwest with her pastor husband and four children.*

* * *

⏱ **For Further Coaching:**

All full links to author websites, articles and blog posts are provided at http://www.nwchristianwriters.org/

- ✓ *"Book Proposals That Sell"* by W. Terry Whalin on The Work of W. Terry Whalin: Dedicated to the Craft of Writing.

- ✓ Jeff Herman and Deborah Levine Herman, *Write the Perfect Book Proposal: 10 That Sold and Why* (Hoboken, NJ: John Wiley & Sons, 2001).

- ✓ Michael Hyatt Intentional Leadership wrote *"Write a Book Proposal That Leaves Publishers Begging to Publish You."*

- ✓ *Writers Conference Guidelines: Helping Writers Master the Submission Process* lists helpful articles under the topic "Book Proposals" including *"A Book Proposal to Grab an Editor"* by Susan Osborn.

- ✓ *"How to Write a Book Proposal"* by Rachelle Gardner, agent for Books & Such Literary Agency.

- ✓ Terry Burns, agent for Hartline Literary Agency, blogged, *"Can I Sell on Proposal?"*

- ✓ *"Nonfiction Book Proposal Cheat Sheet"* posted by Lilly Ghahremani & Stefanie Von Borstel of Full Circle Literary.

What Goes on a One Sheet?

by Erica Vetsch

One of the big facets of preparation for a writing conference is the one sheet/pitch sheet/sell sheet. This piece of paper goes by a lot of names, and it causes consternation and fear in unpublished authors. Basically, it's a sheet of paper that tells what you've written and why you think it is cool. It's used during your agent or editor appointments or if you happen to have a moment with an agent, editor, mentor, or otherwise interested party. It helps you organize your thoughts and gives you something to refer to so your hands won't shake.

Often I hear the question, "What goes on a one sheet?"

I will show you the one sheet I used to help sell my first novel. I'll walk you through what I put on it, and you can see the actual one sheet on lineat the link provided in the introduction section of the book. Look for the links to: Page 1 (the front), and page 2 (the back).

I created my one sheet using a newsletter template from Microsoft and Microsoft Publisher 2007. By fiddling with the colors and the text boxes, I arrived at a layout I liked so much that I've continued to use it for each one sheet I've prepared since.

I chose to use the front and the back of the sheet. The information on the back helps focus the book specifically for the publisher I was targeting.

On the front:

- A picture illustrates the book's theme, historical era, and gives the flavor of the story.
- Contact information for agent and myself.
- Story genre and word count.
- A hook line.
- The title of the work and the author's name again.
- A brief summary.
- Very brief character GMCs (Good Moral Character).
- Author photo and brief bio.

On the back:

- The title and author again.
- Setting of the story. Because this was targeted

at Heartsong Presents, the editor wanted to see several pieces. One is the setting, in this case, historical Minnesota. I described the historical event that spawned the story.

- Bible verse. Heartsong Presents has a Bible verse(s) the spiritual theme centers on.

- Spiritual takeaway. A brief overview of the lesson that will be learned or the change that will take place in the main characters in the story.

It helps you organize your thoughts and gives something to refer to so your hands won't shake

- Series development ideas. A brief synopsis of potential story ideas for the series along with potential titles.

- Manuscript status. Tell editors or agents the manuscript is available, or give them an accurate idea of how long it would take you to get a manuscript to them.

- Another photo. This one is of the actual ship that wrecked. I first got the story idea from this photo.

Do you need a pitch sheet to sell a novel? No, not at all. I just happen to like them. I also like that I use the same format for each so I can quickly find the information I'm looking for, even when I'm nervous or the question is unexpected.

Will editors take your one sheet with them? Not always, though in the appointments I've had, editors have made notes on the one sheet and taken it.

How long does it take to create a one sheet? The answer depends on the writer. One sheets express the creativity of each writer and present the vision they have for their book.

* * *

Erica Vetsch *writes historical romance set in the American West. She loves history, museums, and fiction that sweeps her away into another time and place. You can find her online at* http://onthewritepath.blogspot.com/.

* * *

🕐 For Further Coaching:

All full links to author websites, articles and blog posts are provided at http://www.nwchristianwriters.org/

- ✓ "*Sample One Sheet*" of author Beth K. Vogt posted on the Oregon Christian Writers website.

- ✓ Suzanne Hartman posted "*Creating a One-Sheet*" on her blog, *Write This Way*.

- ✓ "*Christian Writing 101: How to Create a One-sheet for Writers or Speakers*" by Tracy Ruckman on *Christian Writing Examiner.*

- ✓ Romance Writers on the Journey featured "*What's a One Sheet?*" by author and blog host Keli Gwyn.

Ready, Set, Go - to a Writers Conference

by Lydia E. Harris

"Go to a writers conference soon," a seasoned author advised when I began writing. I followed her counsel and learned that conferences are essential for both beginning and experienced writers.

To gain the most from a conference, here's how to prepare.

Get Ready: Choose Classes

When the conference brochure arrives or is posted online, study it, and choose a continuing class if offered. You'll find classes for various genres, such as fiction, nonfiction, and poetry, as well as classes on writing basics, advanced writing, and marketing techniques. Research the classes and teachers, evaluate your writing needs, and pray about the choices. Still can't decide? Seek advice from fellow writers or the conference director.

I did so for my first conference fifteen years ago. The director said, "You can't go wrong with the class on article writing." She was right. Not only did I learn plenty, but I also bought the instructor's tapes to review the class.

Now, years later, I still pray for God's guidance about classes and often ask others for input. "Many advisers make victory sure" (Proverbs 11:14). Once you're at the conference, if your class choice doesn't meet your needs, ask to change to another one (if there's room). However, sometimes when a class seems like the wrong choice at first, it turns out to be God's choice.

Conferences also offer dozens of workshops. Although you may not need to make definite decisions about them until you're there, it's helpful to gather information and make tentative choices beforehand.

With possibly six to eight workshops offered at once, how do you choose? Study descriptions and note who teaches them. Often I select workshops taught by editors and publishers I'd like to meet. By attending their classes, I learn valuable tips about writing for their publications.

Not all workshops cover writing topics. Some, such as those on prayer, may help you grow spiritually. Others may even help you personally. For example, although I don't write for children, I attended a children's writing workshop to gain tips to improve letters to my grandchildren. An unexpected bonus came when I learned that children's magazines include short features, such as puzzles and recipes. Now I regularly submit recipes to them.

Even if you can't attend every workshop and class, you can often purchase recordings of these sessions and continue learning after the conference.

Select Editors and Agents

Most conferences offer appointments to talk with magazine and book editors, publishers, and agents. To select which ones to meet with, determine your writing interests and abilities, and match them with the needs of the professionals attending.

You will feel more confident when you make appointments and pitch your ideas if you've prepared and organized your writing beforehand

To discover your specific interests and goals, consider: Do you want to write fiction or nonfiction? For children, teens, or adults? For men, women, or families? For magazines or books? Also think about your writing style. Is it academic and intellectual, encouraging and homey, or do you prefer teaching and exhorting? Assess your writing strengths as well. Do you prefer writing short pieces to achieve quick success or long projects that take time and perseverance?

After you understand your strengths and goals, learn all you can about the editors, publishers, and agents attending. To research their publishing needs, study information in the conference brochure, the publications' or agents' websites, and the *Christian Writers' Market Guide*. If you find editors and agents who match your interests, sign up for appointments with them. If you don't wish to make appointments, you'll still gain much from attending the conference. At my first one, I improved my writing skills, learned how the industry worked, and made new friends.

If you're unable to get appointments with editors or agents because they have full schedules, you can meet them during breaks and mealtimes. They attend conferences to discover new writers and want to network with you.

Also, if you attend workshops taught by editors and agents, you'll learn about them and their publishing needs. And if you're attending a local conference, you can meet out-of-town faculty by transporting them back and forth to their hotels. That's how I met my current agent.

Get Set: Prepare Manuscripts

After you determine which industry professionals you want to meet with, consider what you have written or could write before the conference to show them. In the past, I've targeted several publications and gathered specific articles for them. To get organized, I prepared a separate two-pocket folder for each one and labeled it with the publication's name. Inside, I included my resume, a list of article ideas that might match the magazine, and copies of articles to present.

During appointments, I showed editors my manuscripts and noted their responses. I sold several articles on the spot and learned why others didn't suit their needs. "This was very productive," one editor said after he scanned my manuscripts. He asked me to submit several after the conference.

If the folder system doesn't work for you, try a three-ring binder or large envelopes to organize your manuscripts.

For book projects, I prepared a colored, plastic folder for each idea. These expandable folders are large enough to hold numerous pages of a project and other show-and-tell materials. If you have several book ideas, bring one-page overviews of all of them in case the editor isn't interested in the first one you pitch. When this happened to me, I quickly switched to another idea and was invited to submit a book proposal on that topic.

If you plan to speak with agents, prepare a folder with your writing resume, published clips, and one-page overviews of book projects. You will feel more confident when you make appointments and pitch your ideas if you've prepared and organized your writing beforehand.

Go: Plan to Attend

Pray for God's guidance as you plan and prepare for a conference. Then go with an open mind, a teachable spirit, and a flexible attitude. During the conference, continue praying for divine appointments, and look for ways to bless others, not simply to gain help for yourself. Then watch God work as you learn and make connections.

* * *

Lydia E. Harris, *MA in Home Economics, has attended numerous writers conferences and teaches at them. She has accumulated hundreds of bylines, contributed to 17 books, and writes a bimonthly column titled **"A Cup of Tea with Lydia."** Her five grandkids call her "Grandma Tea," and together they* *develop and test recipes that are published in* **Focus on the Family** *magazines. Lydia wrote the practical and inspiring Bible study,* **Preparing My Heart for Grandparenting.**

✻ ✻ ✻

⏱ **For Further Coaching:**

All full links to author websites, articles and blog posts are provided at http://www.nwchristianwriters.org/

- ✓ *"Three Necessities for a Writers Conference"* by Kaye Dacus on her site Kay Dacus: Humor, Hope, and Happily Ever Afters.

- ✓ Janet Kobobel Grant, President and Founder of Books & Such Literary Agency, published *"Choosing an Agent."*

- ✓ *"How Not to Get an Agent!"* written by Linda Glaz of Hartline Literary Agency.

- ✓ Katharine Russell, eHow Contributor, wrote *"How to Prepare for a Writer's Conference."* For more information see *"Literary & Publishing Careers."*

- ✓ *"Four Keys for Writers Conference Success"* by Marita Littauer on *Right Writing.*

- ✓ *"For the Conference First-Timer"* by Christina Berry Tarabochia, award-winning author, member of Oregon Christian Writers and speaker for OCW Summer Conference.

During a
Writers
Conference

Make the Most of Your Editor/Agent Appointment

by Melissa K. Norris

You've invested in your writing career and signed up for the conference. You're excited to pitch your manuscript to an editor or an agent. This is it. They're going to love your pitch and request the full manuscript. Your dreams are about to come true, you hope.

Here are some tips to turn that hope into reality:

Finish Your Book

If you are still an unpublished author, the first step is to finish your book. Editors won't buy an unfinished book from a debut author, and agents can't sell what's not written. If your book isn't finished, then you can sit in and gain experience while listening to others pitch.

Check Out Editor and Agent Websites

See what each editor and agent represents and which ones fit your genre and style. Don't pitch your young adult novel to an agent who clearly states on his site that he only works with adult fiction. Spend time following his blog. You'll receive an education in the publishing business and get a feel for the editor's or agent's style. This is especially important for an agent. You'll be working with your agent, hopefully, for the length of your career, so you want to make sure your personalities are compatible. You can glean a lot from the tone of his blog and how he interacts with reader comments.

Write Your Pitch Down and Practice

This is the perfect time to pull out your query and utilize the best of it. Take your pitch with you to the appointment. If you get so nervous you can't remember your own name, you can read from your notes. Your pitch should include the information from your one sheet, which is a one-line description of your book and a couple of paragraphs that read much like the back-cover copy on a novel.

Start Off with Your Name, Genre, and Word Count

"My name is Melissa K. Norris, and my novel is a 90,000-word historical romance titled, *A Pioneer Heart*."

Be Open to Comments and Feedback

Sometimes editors or agents will offer comments on your pitch. Do not, I repeat, do not argue with them. You may not agree with what they say. But if you appear to be unteachable at the first meeting, they won't ask to see anything else from you, no matter how great your pitch was. If they don't ask you to send your manuscript, it's fine to ask them for any tips they might have to strengthen your pitch.

See what each editor and agent represent and which ones fit your genre and style

Bring Copies of Your Proposal

Bring copies of your proposal and the first three chapters. But don't hand them to editors or agents unless they ask for them. Most will prefer you e-mail them the information once they've gotten home. If they took everyone's papers, they wouldn't be able to fit their clothes into their suitcases. But sometimes they'll ask for this material, and you want to be prepared.

Send the Requested Information

If an editor or agent requests your work, then send it. Make sure you give it another final edit. You'll probably want to apply the great things you've learned from the conference to your work. But do send it.

Relax

Editors and agents are people. For an agent's perspective on pitching appointments, see links below.

✳   ✳   ✳

Melissa K. Norris *is a novelist, newspaper columnist, and author of* **Pioneering Today: Faith and Home the Old-Fashioned Way.** *Visit her website to inspire your faith and pioneer roots.* http://www.melissaknorris.com *She is also co-owner of TriLink, a social media mentoring company.* http://www.trilink-social-media.com.

✳   ✳   ✳

🕐 **For Further Coaching:**

All full links to author websites, articles and blog posts are provided at http://www.nwchristianwriters.org/

- ✓ *"What to Expect from Your Editor"* and *"Working with the Editor"* by Meg Schneider and Barbara Doyen on Netplaces.

- ✓ *"Publishing Advice from Jeanette Perez of HarperCollins Publishers"* by Ginny Wiehardt on *About.com Fiction Writing*.

- ✓ The Editor's Blog posted *"Duties of an Editor & How Editors Help Writers"* by fiction editor Beth Hill.

- ✓ *"How to Pitch Agents at a Writers Conference"* on Writers Digest: Write Better Get Published by Chuck Sambuchino.

- ✓ Sue Fagalde Lick wrote *"The Perfect Pitch: Pitching to Agents at a Writing Conference"* on Writing World.

Be Selfish. Volunteer.

By Kim Vandel

Maybe you've thought about volunteering at a writers conference but decided you couldn't possibly fit one more thing into your schedule. It's true that volunteering requires an investment of time and energy, but it's not all *give* and no *take*. In fact, it's a lot more *take* than *give*.

While you won't get paid, volunteers usually receive some compensation. It could be a free CD of a workshop, a "volunteer" ribbon for your name tag, or the eternal gratitude of a frazzled conference director. Whatever form it comes in, you'll be rewarded for your efforts.

Volunteering is also a great way to break the ice at conferences. Its's networking introverts

Volunteering is also a great way to break the ice at conferences. It's networking for introverts. I know it's a lot easier for me to put myself out there when it's part of my job. Having an excuse to strike up a conversation eases anxiety and the awkwardness of talking to total strangers.

When you talk to people, you learn things. The publishing world thrives on information, and people involved with writers conferences are "in the know." Volunteer positions give you access to a variety of professionals in the industry—published authors, marketing experts, agents, editors, and more. You'll come across all kinds of useful information you won't find anywhere else. A two-minute conversation could save you hours of frustrating Internet research.

If you have extra opportunities to talk with editors or agents, they're more likely to remember you and the project you pitched during your appointment. Even if it turns out that they aren't interested in your project, you're making an important connection that could pay off later. Maybe the editor will be interested in your next project or the agent can point you in the direction of someone who *is* interested in what you write.

Volunteering also sends a message to editors and agents that you take the writing business seriously. If you're sacrificing your valuable time, then you probably won't waste *their* valuable time by pitching a project you'll never follow through on.

Time is a precious commodity, and we want to make every minute count. We want to make every dollar count too, especially the money we invest in a writers conference. A lack of volunteers can limit the number of workshops offered, but with plenty of help, a conference director can include a wider variety of options for attendees. More volunteers translates into more presenters, more workshops, and more agents and editors taking appointments. More value for your time and money.

Volunteering also sends a message to editors and agents that you take the writing business seriously

When you work side by side with someone at a writers conference, camaraderie develops. Often the people you volunteer with turn into friends. In an industry filled with rejection, it helps to have plenty of friends who understand what you're going through and who can provide encouragement.

Having the opportunity to encourage those friends in return helps us keep things in perspective. As much as we don't want to admit it, we're not the center of the universe. We live in a society obsessed with self, and we get sucked into it more often than we'd like. Volunteering helps us break away from the "me" mentality. It's more fulfilling and less stressful than a constant focus on self. So really, giving to others benefits *you* in the end.

You'll feel good about yourself when you give your time as a volunteer. People will be impressed. They'll think you worked really hard without getting paid a single penny when the truth is that most volunteer positions are mind-numbingly easy. It's enough to make you feel guilty.

If you've never considered volunteering at a writers conference, ask others about their experiences. Most will agree that you get a lot more out of it than you put in. If you've thought about volunteering but have never taken that step, I encourage you to jump in, and give it a try. It's a small investment with a huge payoff. You can contribute to a worthy cause, give your writing career a boost, and make yourself look good at the same time.

So go ahead. Be selfish. Volunteer.

Kim Vandel *wanted to be Princess Leia when she grew up, but she's decided that being a writer is even better than leading a rebellion against the Empire. Her current project is a young adult urban fantasy novel set in Washington State. It features plenty of coffee but no vampires. You can find her book reviews and more at* www.kimvandel.com.

* * *

⏰ **For Further Coaching:**

All full links to author websites, articles and blog posts are provided at http://www.nwchristianwriters.org/

- ✓ "*Recruiting Volunteers for Christian Ministries*" on Ministry Tools Resource Center.

- ✓ Read Help Others, a portal dedicated to small acts of kindness.

- ✓ The website Helping Quotes is filled with words to inspire.

✓ *"Bible Verses About Serving: 20 Helpful Scriptures Quotes"* published by Pamela Rose Williams on What Christians Want to Know: Topics to Equip, Encourage and Energize.

Conference Networking

by Mindy Peltier

All writers dream of being discovered. You imagine your precious words, birthed in the agony known only to mothers and writers, displayed in bookstores and libraries. Your thoughts might wander past book publication to speaking engagements, book signings, TV appearances, and fame. Publication would surely justify the lost sleep, mountains of dirty laundry, and the forgotten hobbies.

Dreams are good, if rooted in reality. When fueled by unrealistic expectations, you might attend a writers conference, hoping every contact will help rocket you to stardom. With this mind-set, you might view people as stepping-stones toward your goals or as useless stones to toss in the river. Realistic expectations come from understanding the roles others play in the path to publication.

Networking *is* a crucial part of any career or ministry. But it's deeper than fostering relationships with people in the industry to gain personal advantage. Christian networking is being divinely led. At a writers conference, you can draw from a vast pool of wisdom, experience, knowledge, and encouragement. A networking plan of faith grounds your heart in reality and provides the best outcome.

Pray

Relinquish your expectations as you pray specifically about the conference. "Commit to the Lord whatever you do, and your plans will succeed" (Proverbs 16:3 NIV). You offer your gift of writing to him, and he establishes a plan to use it. Pray for the staff, the workshops you plan to attend, and for fellow attendees. Ask for a heart sensitive to the Lord's direction. On a path prepared with prayer, you'll see the Lord's leading as you network.

Pursue

Pursue relationships. Smile, introduce yourself, and hand out business cards at appropriate times. At meals and in workshops, introduce yourself to fellow attendees. Whether you're ready for publication or not, as an opportunity arises, introduce yourself to agents and editors without monopolizing their time. Introduce yourself to workshop presenters, and thank them for their instruction.

When I attended my first Northwest Christian Writers Association meeting, I was nervous. For the first time in over twenty years, I wasn't walking into a room as a homeschooling mommy of six or Scott's wife. I was Mindy, the writer. Usually a confident, outgoing person, I experienced shyness. I clamped my arms to my side to hide my damp fear. Nobody introduced themselves. I repeated, "Hi, I'm Mindy." "Hi, I'm Mindy."

The second month, I repeated this routine. I greeted a few members by name and asked about their writing projects. Still,

Networking gathers a writer's most valuable assets–people

nobody approached me. By the third meeting, I wanted to quit, but my passion to write pushed me through the doors one more time. I needed these people. This time, people responded. They remembered me. They smiled. I introduced myself into their lives, and NCWA became my home.

My mistake was expecting all writers to be outgoing like me. I've learned that the majority are introverts, more comfortable writing than meeting and greeting. Now, as a board member of NCWA and a volunteer for the Northwest Christian Writers' Renewal, I enjoy greeting new writers, especially those with arms tightly clamped to their sides. I know their secret.

Whether you're an introvert or extrovert, pursue relationships. Networking gathers a writer's most valuable assets—people.

Purpose

You must understand the purpose of the people in your network. These relationships are like Christmas; it's about getting and giving.

Christian writers are not your competition; they're your potential friends, prayer partners, critique partners, or coauthors. You will gain much from others, but even a beginning writer can find ways to serve others. Be humble in learning, faithful in promoting, and generous in encouragement.

Agents and editors aren't there to hinder your goals or to place you on a Christian pedestal. Their *There's more to being a writer than putting words on paper* responsibility is to print the instructions and inspiration the church needs *and* keep their businesses profitable. Glean their wisdom in workshops and conversation. Whether or not they publish you, extend your prayer and respect.

At conferences, you meet amazing people. Some will bless you with their gifts; others will be blessed by your gifts. Such divine encounters glorify the Giver of all good gifts.

Patience

It takes time to grow a writer. The various paths to maturity may converge further down the road than you planned.

On the spiritual path, the Lord perfects us through life experiences. Most writers have suffering in common. Writing is crucial to our healing, but healing is also crucial to our writing. Ultimately, spiritual growth comes from faithfully studying God's Word and abiding through joys and sorrows.

Your craft path includes more than just writing skills. Today's writer needs proficiency in public speaking and marketing. Even prolifically published writers continually increase their skill set.

The path of personal maturity may be the one you have the least control over. Your family schedule might not be ready for the demands of a book contract. Health challenges could be stealing your writing time and draining your energy.

When Judy Bodmer attended her first conference, she didn't know eight years would pass before her book, *When Love Dies: How to Save a Hopeless Marriage,* would be published. Now she understands the Lord's timing: she needed to be prepared for television appearances, radio interviews, and a public-speaking ministry.

Judy said, "If the book came out when I went to my first conference, I wouldn't have been able to handle it. A writer has to grow professionally and personally. Don't push your writing skills ahead of personal growth. There's more to being a writer than putting words on paper." Not only is Judy published, but she also directs the Northwest Christian Writers' Renewal.

Be patient as the Lord matures your gifts and abilities; you will bear ripe fruit in his time.

Peace

The networking plan that began with prayer ends with peace. You can trust the Lord for the outcome of the conference with a quiet confidence the secular world doesn't always experience. "And the peace of God, which transcends all understanding, will guard your hearts and your minds in Christ Jesus" (Philippians 4:7). The Lord called you, is equipping you, and will use your gifts according to the plan he established.

Now, close your eyes, rest peacefully on your realistic expectations, and dream.

Remember that dream where you get published?

* * *

Mindy Peltier *was a reporter and columnist for the Cavalier County Republican during high school in North Dakota. She has blogged over a thousand posts about her life as a Christian homeschooling mom, grandma, thyroid-cancer patient, and writer at In the Write Moment. She serves on the board of directors for the Northwest Christian Writers Association and is a member of the Oregon Christian Writers. You can find Mindy online at* www.mommamindy.wordpress.com.

* * *

For Further Coaching:

All full links to author websites, articles and blog posts are provided at http://www.nwchristianwriters.org/

- ✓ "*The Surrendered Writing Career*" by Nick Harrison, Senior Editor at Harvest House Publishers.

- ✓ W. Terry Whalin on his blog, The Writing Life, instructed to "*Keep Building Publishing Relationships*."

- ✓ "*24 Networking Tips that Actually Work*" from Passive Panda.

Winding Up Your Pitch
Prepare to Pitch to Agents and Editors at a Writers Conference

by Amy Letinsky

Your pitch can make or break your meetings with agents and editors at a writers conference. What is a pitch? It is a condensed description of your writing project that you present to editors and agents. The purpose of a pitch is to share your ideas with editors and agents who are looking for new material and writers.

Just as many different types of pitches are thrown in baseball, many types of pitches are also delivered at writers conferences. There are short pitches and long pitches. The style of the pitch also changes depending on the type of material you are presenting.

The Elevator Pitch

The shortest type of pitch is known as the *elevator pitch* because it is short enough to deliver between floors on an elevator. This pitch is for those brief interactions with editors and agents where you have their full and undivided attention for a limited amount of time. I do not recommend following them into the bathrooms to deliver this kind of pitch, but you might find an occasion to speak with them in the hallway between sessions or when you encounter them in the lunch line.

Elevator pitches range from a few seconds to a minute long. You will provide only key information about your writing, enough to get them asking for more. Tantalize them with your best stuff, the interesting facts you have discovered (nonfiction), or the insurmountable conflict between your main characters (fiction). Briefly introduce yourself, your background, and your platform. Then explain why you are uniquely suited to write this material.

Do not count on your spontaneous wit to see you through. This type of pitch, more than any other, demands practice and precision.

Northwest Christian Writers Association's own best-selling author James Rubart has provided examples of enticing elevator pitches for his novels:

Rooms: "A young Seattle software tycoon inherits a home on the Oregon coast that turns out to be a physical manifestation of his soul."

The purpose of a pitch is to share your ideas with editors and agents who are looking for new material and writers

Book of Days: "A man who is losing the memories of his late wife goes on a quest to find God's Book of Days described in Psalm 139:16 that has recorded the past, present, and future of every soul on earth."

The Chair: "What if you were given a chair made by Christ that might have supernatural healing powers and it could heal the life you destroyed twelve years ago?"

Soul's Gate: "What if you could send your spirit into other people's souls to fight for their healing and freedom?"

The Editor/Agent Appointment Pitch

The length of these pitches depends on several variables. Some editor/agent appointments at conferences are one-on-one, and for some, you will be in a group with other writers who will be sharing their ideas during the same time slot. Depending on how many people are sharing, you could have anywhere from two to ten minutes. That is a big difference in time, so you should plan for all kinds of variations.

It might help to write out your most important points first, which are often those covered in your elevator pitch. Then create a list of additional information that could be helpful in order of most importance, so you can incorporate it as time allows. Another possibility is crafting a two-minute pitch, a five-minute pitch, and a ten-minute pitch, just to have a template to work with when you are on the spot. And while it is best to memorize your pitch, a simple outline can be handy to guide you.

Do not forget that editors will often interrupt you to ask questions, so be prepared to give further details on specific items in your pitch and possibly abandon other information that you intended to cover. Your goal is to provide the information that they want to hear.

What Every Pitch Needs

Certain elements are essential to every pitch:

- **Customize for each specific publisher or agent.**

- This will require homework on your part, but you need to know what material these publishers and agents are seeking and what they typically publish and represent.

- **Specify your target audience.**

- Make sure you clarify the age group you are targeting and what gender is more likely to read your work. Any additional specific demographics also help.

But when you come prepared, you will stand out from the rest of the crowd for organizing your ideas and presenting them in a meaningful way

- **Describe how your work is both unique but also similar to others.**

- "There is nothing new under the sun" (Eccles. 1:9 NIV), so do not try to claim complete uniqueness. Instead, recognize the big names doing similar things, and explain how your ideas add to the important ongoing discussion about your topic.

- **Give the length.**

- Editors and agents often speak in terms of word counts as opposed to page counts, but both numbers are helpful to have on hand. Be aware of the lengths of other similar books or articles, and be prepared to make comparisons.

- **Tell your qualifications and platform.**

- When you pitch, you are not only pitching your ideas, but you also are pitching yourself. Your expertise and qualifications help sell the writing. In addition, your platform informs the editor or agent about your capacity to self-promote.

Nonfiction Book-and-Article Pitches

The most important component of a nonfiction pitch is your thesis: your main point. But you might not lead the pitch with this information, as your platform or interesting statistics might be a better draw. Tell the editor or agent about your unique approach to the material. Do you focus on a lot of facts and statistics, or do you rely on personal experiences and stories to make your points? What is your general tone: humorous, serious, or deeply spiritual? For articles, show off your knowledge of their publication by indicating for what section you think the article might be best suited.

Fiction Book Pitches

While it is tempting to start at the beginning of your story and walk your audience through it scene by scene, you will fail to fit in all the required information for the pitch. Instead, focus on key characters and conflicts to give the editor or agent a taste for the story. Make sure you mention your genre, as there is a big difference in publishers' and agents' minds between chick lit and romance.

When pitching her novels, Lesley Ann McDaniel, author of the soon-to-be-released *Lights, Cowboy, Action*, has found success when using a common formula: "When opening conflict happens to main character(s), they have to overcome conflict by completing the quest."

Pitching your writing at a conference for the first time can be a nerve-wracking experience. But when you come prepared, you will stand out from the rest of the crowd for organizing your ideas and presenting them in a meaningful way.

✳ ✳ ✳

Amy Letinsky *has successfully pitched fiction and nonfiction books as well as articles at writers conferences. She is a college writing and literature instructor and blogger.* Read *more of her writing tips at* <u>amyletinsky.wordpress.com</u>.

✳ ✳ ✳

⏱ **For Further Coaching:**

All full links to author websites, articles and blog posts are provided at http://www.nwchristianwriters.org/

- ✓ Writers Conference Guidelines: Helping Writers Master the Submission Process posted "*Getting Your Pitch Right*."

- ✓ The Steve Laube Agency blogged "*The Wild Pitch*" by Steve Laube and "*Do You Have the Perfect Pitch?*" by Karen Ball.

- ✓ "*Pitching Your Book Proposal*" by Dr. Dennis E. Hensley, director of Taylor University's Professional Writing program.

Pitching with Perfection

by Michelle Hollomon

We sat around a table waiting for our turns to pitch our projects to the publishing-house editor. We pinned our hopes to the moments when we would either be cheering or choking. It was the beginning of my writers conference experiences, and I felt the weight of the literary world on my shoulders as I anticipated my turn. The pressure was on. *Will I grab her attention?* I wondered. *Will I sound stupid, egotistical, or insecure?*

The editor handed business cards to the lucky ones and invited them to send their proposals to her. The unlucky ones received good wishes for better luck next time.

Pitching is a curious way to describe what we writers do with editors and agents. We basically present our ideas for sale

I've never seen rude or condescending editors or agents in the Christian publishing arena. On the contrary, they have been professional, courteous, and helpful. But rejection is rejection, and simply nothing about it feels good. On this particular occasion, I experienced the "better luck next time" scenario. It wouldn't be my last.

A lot of years and pitching opportunities have come and gone since then, and I've learned a few things. Pitching is a curious way to describe what we writers do with editors and agents. We basically present our ideas for sale. Instead of using the word *pitching*, we could call it *diving* or *plunging* or *falling head over heels*. For me it always feels like jumping off a cliff and waiting for my wings to catch a draft.

Here are some things to keep in mind as you give your perfect pitch:

Be Concise

Boil your project down, and start with your *essence sentence*. What is the most important thing? If you could use only one sentence, how would you describe it? Here are some examples of essence sentences:

- God is better than we think, but past "god figures" in our lives have left us with less than perfect ways to think about him.

> *For me it always feels like jumping off a cliff and waitng for my wings to catch a draft*

- Sixteenth-century Rome was corrupt with a power-hungry Pope, but when a cardinal hired an unsuspecting young woman as his personal poisoner, the Vatican would never be the same.

Be Confident

Try to forget about yourself, and let your idea do the talking. Believe in your idea so much that you get out of its way and let it have its voice. You're not pitching you; you're pitching your God-breathed idea.

Be Informed

Know to whom you are talking and what they are looking for. If the editors or agents are looking for young-adult fiction, don't pitch your devotional. Research those who may be most interested in your project, and go directly to them.

Breathe

This cannot be emphasized enough. Take three to five deep breaths before you begin talking to deliver oxygen to your brain and calm your body. You may not be able to quiet your mind, but you can quiet your body.

Be Yourself

Acquisition editors and literary agents are not a different breed or class. They are ordinary people with ordinary jobs that offer extraordinary opportunities. Those opportunities come in the form of writers like you and me. They are as interested in hearing our ideas as we are in sharing them. Instead of focusing on impressing them, focus on learning from them.

Be Inquisitive

In addition to sharing your project, ask for suggestions. This feedback can be pure gold. It may be the very thing your manuscript needs to move it to the next level. The feedback I've received from publishing professionals, even short snippets, has shaped my writing into what it is today.

Be Enthused

There is no mistaking sincere enthusiasm for your own project. If you are passionate about your project and its

You're not pitching you; you're pitching your God-breathed idea

intended impact on your target audience, don't hesitate to share that energy with agents and editors. They may sit all day listening to writers. Why not stand out for being thrilled about your project? If editors or agents like your idea, they'll need to catch some of that enthusiasm to sell it to the rest of their publishing team. It's important to not only make an impression by your enthusiasm but also to make a friend who can share the vision with you.

Be Prepared

Some simple steps will help you *be* prepared and *feel* prepared:

1. Write your pitch down several times until it is concise, refined, and boiled down to its essence. Like an expensive perfume, you want to leave editors and agents with a positive and professional association between you and your work.

2. Practice giving your pitch. You don't have to memorize the whole thing, but you may want to memorize the two or three unique points you want to hit.

3. If you don't have a web camera or a smart phone with video ability, find a teenager, and video yourself giving the pitch. Do you seem bored, disinterested, insecure, or energetic and confident? If you don't know, ask that handy teenager what he thinks.

4. Use the power of imagination. Once you're prepared, take a minute to imagine yourself successfully delivering the pitch and receiving warm interest and appreciation from those who hear it.

In Case You Freak Out

Just ask to start over. Smile, breathe, and then present your project like you practiced. I've had to do this myself, and I was afraid what the people around the table were thinking about me. But they were glad it happened to me and not to them! We all know how it feels to be nervous. Others want you to succeed. Your important project can only fulfill its divine purpose if you present it clearly. Take the risk, and reap the rewards.

❋ ❋ ❋

Michelle Hollomon *is a licensed counselor and professional coach who has written articles for local and national publication. Her recent book,* **God Unwrapped: God Is Love,**

but Not the Kind You Are Used To (*Harrison House*) *was published in September 2011.*

* * *

🕐 For Further Coaching:

All full links to author websites, articles and blog posts are provided at http://www.nwchristianwriters.org/

- ✓ Brandilyn Collins, in the archives of her blog, *Forensics and Faith*, covered "*Creating a Pitch for Your Book*" and "*Feedback on Pitches*."

- ✓ "*Secrets of a Great Pitch*" published by Rachelle Gardener of Books & Such Literary Agency. She also includes a list of Writing/Publishing Websites for further study.

- ✓ Laura Helmuth advises "*How Not to Pitch*" on the Science writers' website, The Open Notebook.

After a
Writers
Conference

Use Your Prayer Power Tool!

By Lydia E. Harris

Years ago, I sensed a need for prayer. I knew I couldn't complete the writing tasks God gave me without that support. Nor would my writing affect lives without his anointing. So I asked others to pray for me.

Prayer is a powerful tool that impacts our writing and, therefore, our readers. But sometimes it's overlooked. Although we can write words, only God can touch hearts. No matter

> *Prayer is a powerful tool that impacts our writing and, therefore, our readers*

how cleverly we craft sentences, without his blessing, our words are only ink on paper. If you need prayer support, take these steps:

Pray First, Then List Names

Who could pray for you? Ask God. Then consider relatives, friends, church members, and writers. By e-mail, you can contact people around the world.

List individuals who are mature in faith, keep their commitments, and are interested in your writing. The apostle Paul wrote about Timothy, "I have no one else like him, who takes a genuine interest in your welfare" (Philippians 2:20 NIV). Wouldn't it be wonderful to have someone like Timothy on your prayer team?

God provided a dozen faithful prayer warriors for me. They rejoice in my successes and encourage me during setbacks. But mainly, they pray. And that's where the power lies—connecting with God Almighty in prayer.

Contact Potential Prayer Partners

After you've made a list, graciously ask these people to consider joining your prayer team, but give them freedom to say no. Tell them what their commitment would involve and what yours would be. I asked my prayer team to pray for me once a week for one year. In return, I promised to use my writing time wisely and to send regular reports.

Send Writing Updates

Your updates may be weekly, monthly, or as needed. I started with monthly e-mails, but prayer needs came up more often. Now I aim for weekly contacts.

And that's where the power lies— connecting with God Almighty in prayer

In your updates, start with answered prayers. I call this section "Give Thanks" and list ways God helped me. Sharing answers gives God glory and motivates my team to keep praying. One member wrote, "I'm blessed to share a fraction of the action of lives touched through your writing."

Also, God values a grateful heart. Do you remember the story of the ten lepers Jesus healed? When only one returned to thank him, Jesus sorrowfully asked, "Were not all ten cleansed? Where are the other nine?" (Luke 17:17).

I desire to be like the leper who returned to thank God. To help me remember what God did, I print out my updates and put them in a notebook. Then I can look back at previous requests and include answers in the current update. There are numerous ways to record God's answers, so choose one that works for you.

After my "Give Thanks" section, the "Please Pray" portion follows with five or six requests. I list writing, speaking, and teaching needs and may include requests for editors, publishers, and readers.

Express Appreciation

Besides thanking God for your prayer team, it's important to thank them for praying. I often begin updates with, "Thank you for praying." Then I might end with, "Your prayers are a real gift to me."

In addition to thanking them in e-mail messages, occasionally I send thank-you notes or small gifts, such as bookmarks, by regular mail. Thanksgiving, Christmas, and Valentine's Day are good times to mail cards with personal notes. If your prayer team prays while you write a book, list their names in the acknowledgments page, and offer each of them a free copy.

Also, don't assume the prayer warriors will pray forever. Though most of mine have prayed for years, each year I ask if they wish to continue.

Return the Favor

We're not the only ones who need prayer. Pray for your prayer team and other writers. If another writer asks you for prayer support, say yes if possible.

> *I desire to be like the leper who returned to thank God*

As you send updates to your prayer team, sometimes include a written prayer for them. It can be as short as, "May the joy of the Lord be your strength" (based on Nehemiah 8:10).

Prayer is a high calling. Right now "Christ Jesus . . . is at the right hand of God and is also interceding for us" (Romans 8:34). What a privilege to follow his example and pray for others!

Reap the Benefits

I'm grateful God nudged me to form a prayer team. They have prayed for me through joys and tears and through writing a lengthy Bible study for grandparents. Their support not only motivates me to persevere, but it also gives me courage to tackle God-sized projects. Their prayers have blessed me in countless ways.

If you don't already have a prayer team, I encourage you to follow these steps and tap into this divine source of power. Then watch God work!

�֍   �֍   �֍

Lydia E. Harris, *MA in Home Economics, has attended numerous writers conferences and teaches at them. She has accumulated hundreds of bylines, contributed to 17 books, and writes a bimonthly column titled* **"A Cup of Tea with Lydia."** *Her five grandkids call her "Grandma Tea," and together they develop and test recipes that are published in* **Focus on the Family** *magazines. Lydia wrote the practical and inspiring Bible study,* **Preparing My Heart for Grandparenting***.*

�֍   ✷   ✻

🕐 **For Further Coaching**:

All full links to author websites, articles and blog posts are provided at http://www.nwchristianwriters.org/

- ✓ Clubhouse Magazine published "*25 Days of Prayer*" by Lydia Harris.

- ✓ Prayer Coach featured a post called "*Prayer Quotes — A.W. Tozer.*"

- ✓ Focus on the Family posted "*Prayer Has Its Reasons*" by Robert Velarde, author of *Conversations with C.S. Lewis* (InterVarsity Press), *The Heart of Narnia* (NavPress), and *Inside the Screwtape Letters* (Baker Books).

✓ Sandy Tritt, Inspiration for Writers, Inc., wrote *"The Writing Life: A Writer's Prayer."*

✓ *"Plug in Your Power Tool – Prayer!"* by Lydia Harris on the blog, Author Culture.

✓ *"A Writer's Prayer"* was posted by Mary DeMuth, along with free articles on writing, parenting, healing, and social media.

✓ CASA Network: The Christian Association Serving Adult Ministries Network published *"Grandparenting: Giving a Gift that Outlasts Others"* by Lydia Harris.

Presenting Yourself Online the Write Way

By Melissa K. Norris and Janalyn Voigt
writing for TriLink Social Media Mentoring

You've pitched your book idea and hit a home run. The editor or agent you met with has asked to see your project. You refrain from doing a Snoopy dance, express your thanks, and float through the rest of the conference. As soon as you arrive home you'll give your manuscript a final once-over with all the new editing tips you've learned and send it off as *requested material*.

In the hallway, you hear an agent tell someone she always does an Internet search for an author's name when she receives their material. Your pulse kicks up a notch. What's this? She'll be checking out your online presence before even reading your book? Is your online presence strong enough? Will she like what she sees?

No need to panic. There are plenty of ways to make sure your online presence is professional without spending a lot of money or hiring a PR firm.

Author Website

You need to have an author website. It shows you're committed to being a professional author and that you understand the importance of connecting with readers online. The first thing to do is purchase your domain name. Melissa uses *GoDaddy.com* and Janalyn recommends *Hostgator* or *BlueHost* to register and host domain names. We recommend you install a self-hosted *WordPress.org* site, and so does Michael Hyatt. Here is his *twenty minute tutorial* for starting your WordPress blog and website.

What to Put on Your Website

Author photo: You need a good author photo. If you don't care enough to put up a professional photo, then people will automatically assume you won't give professional attention to your writing. This is the one thing we recommend hiring someone to do. Let the photographer know you need your images in digital form and for your website.

About the author page: Show your personality and reflect your genre. Do you write historical fiction? Give some tidbits about your favorite historical facts or places. Do you write humor? Have a few funny lines describing yourself. We recommend writing this section of your website in the first person. You want your readers to feel like they're getting to know you, not reading a formal biography at the back of a book.

Blog: Take time to research blogging before you start. The thought of blogging may make you cringe, and it's not for everyone, but maintaining a blog allows you to connect with your readers. It also provides fresh content for your website, which helps your site's search engine rankings (thus gaining you exposure and possibly, more readers). Take time to think about what you're going to blog and make sure it fits in with your brand and target audience.

Newsletter signup box:
Start building your list right away. Publishers like to see that you have a list in the proposal, which comes before the contract, so start now. We

No need to panic. There are plenty of ways to make your online presence professional

recommend using *MailChimp* for your newsletter needs. They're free up to the first 2,000 subscribers and are easy to use. Even if you don't send out a newsletter right away, you want to start gathering subscribers' email addresses for when you're ready. To protect yourself from anti-spam laws, never sign up anyone for your email list without their permission and always use a double opt-in form.

Contact Page: People need a way to contact you. There are plugins you can activate at your site to help you set up a contact form, or you can put the image of a mailbox on your site that when clicked, allows people to email you. If you're not comfortable using your personal email account, set up a separate one for your professional communications. Also be sure to put up links to your social media sites. Here are tutorials to help you learn how to use WordPress *plugins* and *widgets*. If these instructions are too advanced for you, check our site at http://trilink-social-media.com/.

Social Media Pages

Facebook: Setting up an author Facebook page allows people to "like" you. Using a Facebook profile means you have to accept and send friend requests to connect with others, which as your popularity grows, becomes more time-consuming. Pages allow you to track how your fans engage with and share your content and how they find you. Make sure you use the same photo from your website so people easily know it's the same author. Be sure your posts relate to your genre and are appropriate and professional. (No rants.)

Twitter: Twitter is easy to use and one of the larger social media sites. You can only "tweet" something that is 140 characters long. This forces you to learn how to get to the heart of what you want to say and be concise. Not a bad thing for an author. Using a hashtag (#) before a search word allows you to connect with ongoing conversations. Including hashtags in your tweets extends your reach beyond your own following. Hashtag.org is a site where you can search for hashtags to use.

Goodreads: Goodreads is unique in that it is all about reviewing and discussing books you enjoy. You can see what people like and don't like about books in your genre, participate in book clubs and author discussions, post book reviews, search book lists to see what friends are reading, compile lists of your favorite books, and recommend books to other readers. If you are an author of published books, you can inhabit your author page, upload videos, post excerpts, and host giveaways on Goodreads.

Some Final Thoughts

There are many other social media sites: *LinkedIn*, *GooglePlus*, *Pinterest*, *StumbleUpon,* and more. Find the top two or three that you enjoy the most and focus on building your following there. Using *Google Analytics*, you can see which social media sites drive the most traffic to your website. These are the places to invest your time, because ultimately, you want readers to go to your website. Social media sites come and go. You have no control over that, but you decide whether your website remains online. If your biggest social media site suddenly dies, you want the security of knowing you are engaging with your fans and have captured their contact information at your website.

*   *   *

As **TriLink Social Media Mentors**, *Janalyn Voigt and Melissa K Norris help publishing professionals discover, implement, and market their brands. They partner with those ready to discover their brands, help take existing branding deeper, and customize plans to implement and market brands. They specialize in working with authors who need branding and social media made simple.* http://TriLink-Social-Media.com

*   *   *

🕐 **For Further Coaching:**

All full links to author websites, articles and blog posts are provided at http://www.nwchristianwriters.org/

- ✓ *"Platform Ain't Just for Shoes"* by Ane Mulligan of American Christian Fiction Writers.

- ✓ Jordyn Redwood posted *"Should a Christian Market Themselves?* on American Christian Fiction Writers.

- ✓ *"12 Social Media Essentials For Writers"* by Don Lafferty's Practical Social Media Strategies and Tactics for Connecting with Your Public.

- ✓ Marketing Christian Books: A Personal Guide this Unique Market blogged *"Social Media: Just Do It."*

- ✓ *"How Christian Authors Can Use Twitter"* by Cheri Burbach posted on Rose Allen McCauley, Author: Stories from Small Towns with Huge Hearts.

- ✓ T. Suzanne Eller, a mentor for the Jerry B. Jenkins Christian Writers Guild course, Building Your Social Media Platform, launched a blog series *"Social Media: Does It Work*?" Read through her archives for more information.

- ✓ *"Are you Pinterest Savvy? 1 Million Followers in a Year"* by Melissa K. Norris featured on Wordserve Water Cooler.

✓ *"Social Media and Writers Conferences"* by author Nicole Miller, Social-Media Coordinator OCW Summer Conference. Also see *"How Can I Possibly Keep up with Social Media Trends?"*

The Secret to Getting Published

by Kathleen Freeman

Why You Need a Critique Group

Hands on his hips, he turned his head to look at the group of conference attendees circling him. "Do y'all want to know the secret to getting published?"

He had us. Nobody moved. Nobody breathed as we watched, waiting for the holy grail of writing, the bit of knowledge to move us a rung or two up the ladder of publication. He nodded to the circle. "Find a good critique group."

Some turned away, eyes glazing over. I kept watching, listening. I was in a couple of good critique groups, so I quivered inside to hear that I already had my feet planted on higher rungs.

"Yep," he continued, "that's what my dear wife, Robin Miller, says, and I watched it happen. I watched as she moved from being a great writer to an excellent writer with work everyone clamored to buy. 'Course you have to be willing to put the work into it, to critique and be critiqued regularly."

Maybe the group hoped for an easier step. The rest turned, leaving only me watching, listening. I knew he was right and from more than reading John Gardner's and Raymond Carver's book, *On Becoming a Novelist* (Norton, 1999). I patted my hard-earned rung. I'd been critiquing and having my work critiqued for years, and I learned from the best and the worst. To be honest, the meanest, orneriest varmints taught me the most about critiquing, not because their advice helped my work but because they also showed me how I didn't want to be—belittling, dream-crushing. The fact is that each person, writer or not, has stories to tell, and God has given us unique talents and perspectives to use in that telling.

To polish these diamonds in the rough, we need brave and kind souls to tell us what they like and what isn't working. Sure, self-editing is important, but because they're our stories, we may not see our main characters step out of line or that our dragons materialize out of nowhere. Drafts, self-edited, and read out loud though they might be, are almost always messes. They're like the dream your five-year-old had—very real to him. To you—not so much. An honest reader, even one with no editing experience, will catch problems, saving us from unneeded editors' and agents', uh, "redirections." In the end, your pitch is forgotten, and your writing is what sells the book.

It's a good story. Can't editors and agents see the potential and fix the problems? No doubt. In the publishing world, good isn't enough. Only excellence sells. Turning a rock into a diamond is a huge task, often more work than digging up a new diamond and polishing it themselves. Editors don't tend to undertake such headaches unless your name is Princess Kate or a novel sort of like yours netted five billion dollars.

So what can you do to find help with polishing? You can pay an expert to read your work. Plenty of skilled editors are out there who offer varying degrees of assistance. Prices range from about four-hundred dollars to anywhere in the thousands. They can be worth it—or not. Editors are people, capable of mistakes or glory like everyone else.

For budget feedback options, contests such as the American Christian Fiction Writers (ACFW) Genesis ($35 plus membership) can result in recognition as well. Free or cheap services are also offered through

The fact is that each person, writers or not, has stories to tell, and God has given us unique talents and perspectives to use in that telling

many conferences. Usually, this is for one chapter, a quick look to let you know what needs work and what is spot on.

Most writers' groups, including the Northwest Christian Writers Association (NCWA) and the ACFW, offer help finding a critique group. As the Bible says, "Ask and it will be given to you; seek and you will find" (Matthew

7:7 NIV). Persistence pays. Before you ask where you can sign up, know that you will be expected to critique unto others as you would have them critique unto you. It's a big commitment to help, but writers often learn more from critiquing others' work than from critiques done on their own. Really. "Let us not become weary in doing good, for at the proper time we will reap a harvest if we do not give up" (Galatians 6:9).

So, what should you look for in a critique group? Skill? Passion? Respect? Honesty? Yes. Those are all great. But I've found the most important quality to be commitment. Find or bring together a group of people who realize the climb to publication isn't easy, who place value in helping and receiving help, and who hold on tightly. Before your time to reap comes, you may find yourself praying for your group and invested in their writing careers. They, in turn, can become your greatest advocates in publication. "Therefore encourage one another and build each other up, just as in fact you are doing" (1 Thessalonians 5:11).

✳ ✳ ✳

Kathleen Freeman *spends her days working on novels, articles, editing, and, her passion, helping those around her use their talents to the glory of God. Her work appears in* **Vista: Journal for Holy Living**, *the* **Northwest Christian Author**, **Raising Small Souls**, *and* **Clubhouse** *magazine. She was the 2012 Genesis winner for the young-adult category. She also has several completed novels and a number of works in progress. You can find her online at* www.findinghopeinhardtimes.com.

✳ ✳ ✳

For Further Coaching:

All full links to author websites, articles and blog posts are provided at http://www.nwchristianwriters.org/

- ✓ *"Critique Groups: Support for Your Success"* published by Henry McLaughlin of the Jerry B. Jenkins Christian Writers Guild.

- ✓ W. Terry Whalin encourages *"Join A Critique Group to Get Your Writing Moving."*

- ✓ *"Some Important Steps in Getting Published"* blogged by Joyce Hart, President of Hartline Literary Agency.

Writers' Critique Group Guidelines

by Agnes Lawless Elkins

The purpose of a critique group is to provide mutual encouragement where members can give comments and suggestions to each other that will help improve their manuscripts. A critique group is not a mutual-admiration society nor should a time together be spent in tearing down other writers. Visiting, market news, and announcements should be limited to a reasonable portion of the total time.

The job of critiquers is to encourage the authors and to suggest ways to tighten, clarify, and strengthen their manuscripts. When making comments and recommendations, critiquers should use *I* statements rather than *you* statements.

The job of the author whose manuscript is being discussed is to introduce the manuscript, read it aloud (if members have not already received it ahead of time to critique), listen to comments, ask questions for clarification, and later decide which advice to take.

When You Are Being Critiqued

1. Introduce your manuscript by saying:

   a) What it is: the first draft of a picture book, a short story, the second chapter of a novel, an article, etc.

   b) Who it is for: three-to-five year olds, the women's magazine market, adults, etc.

   c) Do not make excuses such as, "This is really rough."

2. Read or ask someone else to read the manuscript straight through with no digressions or side remarks. You may find yourself circling or underlining problem areas as you hear it read aloud. (In some groups, members hand out, mail, or e-mail copies of their manuscripts to each member to edit at home. At the next meeting, they discuss the critiqued manuscripts.)

3. You may explain the intention or goal of the manuscript in response to the critiques but *may not argue* with the comments.

4. You, the writer, always have the option of setting aside any critiques that you feel do not apply. *This* is *not done verbally*. Remember, it is your manuscript. The final judgment is yours.

When Critiquing

1. Take notes during the reading. (Or if you are critiquing at home, record the notes on your copy of the manuscript. Write your name and the date on your copy, so the author can get back to you if he or she has any questions.)

   a) Be sure the notes are legible and the suggestions are clear. One aid is to put a plus (+) sign by the things you like, a minus sign (-) by the ones you don't, and a question mark (?) where you got confused or didn't understand.

   b) Include the title or chapter number for the convenience of the author. Add your name and date, and hand the notes to the author after the verbal critiques are done.

   c) Give verbal critiques one at a time.

   d) It is okay to ask to see the manuscript or have a short section reread.

2. Be sensitive to feelings.

   a) Start each critique with a positive statement, even if it is only, "This has a lot of promise," "This is better," or "I like your title, . . the humor, . . the phrase . . . "

   b) Don't compare writers.

1. Keep verbal critiques brief and clear. If you have trouble being brief, consider giving only the most important suggestions verbally, then let your notes do the rest.

2. Direct comments toward the work, not the writer. Don't say, "You aren't very good at showing us the character." Instead, say, "I don't see your main character too well." (Exception: "You are very good at dialogue," etc.)

3. The only time you should push for a change is if you are sure the grammar, tense, or punctuation is incorrect. Usually, this is not necessary. If you are unsure, say *so*. It is the writer's job to check it out.

4. Remember, all suggestions are just that, suggestions.

5. *How* they are offered is just as important as *what* is offered. Not, "You can't have a nine year old say that." Instead, "Your hero sounds a little adult to me." The latter is an opinion, and you are entitled to it, but you cannot tell the writer what to do or not do.

> *Remember, we are in critique groups to support each other, bolster each others confidence after rejections letters, and rejoice in each others successes*

6. Do not make a suggestion more than twice, no matter how strongly you feel about it. The writers must take responsibility for the changes, especially those they hear from several people.

7. You don't need to say more than, "I agree with (another critiquer) about __" when someone else has already pointed out a problem or a job well done. Don't go into detail.

What to Listen for

1. **Title:** Is it effective? Does it arouse interest and hint at content?

2. **Beginning:** Does it grab and hold your attention? Does it introduce the information, idea, or personal experience? For fiction, does the story begin at the beginning, or does it start later or earlier than written? Does it introduce the main character and hint of conflict and resolution?

3. **Idea:** Is the premise valid, fresh, and important? Is there a new twist, or has it been overdone? Does the manuscript reflect the author's interest, enthusiasm, and knowledge?

4. **Point of view:** Is it consistent? The right one?

5. **Audience:** Is the writing appropriate for the proposed audience?

6. **Setting:** Do we know where we are? When we

are?

7. **Theme:** Are there too many or too few themes? Is the theme fresh or overdone?

8. **Voice:** Is it fresh, original, and compelling? Age appropriate?

9. **Content:** Does the piece contain extraneous material or digressions? Is the focus sharp? Is sensory detail woven in? Is there too much detail or too little? Does each paragraph add to the author's purpose? Are there enough anecdotes? Too many statistics or quotations? Are the examples pertinent and applicable? If fiction, does the protagonist have a real conflict to solve? Does he or she solve it?

10. **Word choice:** Does the language have clarity, rhythm, and power? Strong verbs and nouns and few adjectives and adverbs? Does it use clichés?

11. **Structure:** Does the manuscript flow well? Is it in logical order, well-paced, and well-organized? Does each word, sentence, and paragraph move the piece forward? Does it have smooth transitions? Is the viewpoint consistent in fiction pieces? Does the plot flow?

12. **Style:** Is the manuscript lively? Does it show rather than tell? Did you notice jolting constructions, jarring words, or redundancies? Is it grammatically correct?

13. **Clarity:** Is the meaning of each sentence and paragraph clear? Do you have to read the passage twice to understand it?

14. **Characters:** Are they well-rounded and believable? Is each one's dialogue distinctive and appropriate to the place, time, and character?

15. **Plot:** Does it develop with credibility and motivations? Has proper foreshadowing been used without giving away the whole story? Do flashbacks lose the reader? Is there sufficient conflict?

16. **Dialogue:** Does it seem natural? Does it advance the story and show character? Do the characters have unique ways of speaking?

17. **Ending:** Is it powerful? Does it make you want to do what the author intends? Is its purpose clear? In fiction works, do the chapter endings make you want to read on? Does the end leave you satisfied?

Helpful Phrases and Suggestions

"You may want to think about . . . "

"Try . . . "

"Consider . . . "

"I agree/disagree with Ann about . . . "

"I wonder if you could strengthen this scene by . . ."

Remember, we are in critique groups to support each other,

bolster each other's confidence after rejections letters, and rejoice in each other's successes.

* * *

Author and copy editor **Agnes Lawless Elkins** *has authored or coauthored eleven books. Her articles have been published in such magazines as* **Decision and Power for Living**. *She was one of the founders of NCWA and is the managing editor of the* **Northwest Christian Author**.

* * *

⊕ For Further Coaching:

All full links to author websites, articles and blog posts are provided at http://www.nwchristianwriters.org/

- ✓ *"Critique Group Guidelines"* published online by the Greater Lehigh Valley Writers Group.

- ✓ Audrey Owen, editor at Writer's Helper, posted *"Writing Group Rules."*

- ✓ *"Starting Your Own Critique Group"* by Margot Finke.

Taking Your Next Steps

by Kim Martinez

The conference is over. Your brain hit overload about fifteen hours in, and now you have more information and ideas than you know what to do with.

How can you make the most of this experience so you propel your writing career forward?

The Creative Pattern (discovered through years of reflection and research) is simple, and it might help you find a place to start:

- Gather information

- Let it germinate

- Organize

- Create

After a conference, you might be tempted to go home and jump right into the creative process. However, you will better set yourself up for success if you follow the Creative Pattern.

Gather Information

Yeah! You already did this. You went to a conference and took a plethora of notes. You probably gathered:

- Presentation handouts and notes

- Business cards from editors/agents

- Business cards from other writers

- Books you want to buy

- Inspired thoughts you haven't jotted down yet

In moments of pause, let your mind offload information for future retrieval. Take time the last day of the conference to begin jotting down those extra ideas.

Make sure to note on the back of the business card or in your meeting notes anything you promised to deliver.

Let It Germinate

Germinating is the act of letting a seed begin to grow. When you get home from the conference, chances are high that you will be hit with life. Yes, Junior did

Only about 5 percent of people who promise something to an editor or agent at a conference actually follow through

throw up three times today; the drier is on the fritz; and "Honey, did you remember to pay the phone bill?"

The first step in a germination process is to let the seed sit, sometimes in a dark place. Don't worry about losing everything you learned at the conference. Let the ideas and thoughts sit in the back of your mind while you take care of essentials—which include rest, exercise, and nutrition.

Keep a notebook close by, because as thoughts pop up, you want to easily record them. The goal is to let your mind relax, the information gel, and then capture the best ideas as they float to the top.

Organize

After a day or two of germination, you will be ready to sit down and develop a plan of approach.

Start with people.

- Who did you meet? Take time to follow up on social media with any new friends.

- Touch base with those you added to your prayer list.

- Who did you promise something to? Make a pile of everything you promised so you can follow up quickly.

Now, organize the information. For starters, make three piles:

- Old information

- New information

- Interesting information to spark ideas for future articles

Throw away the old-information pile. The creative process often collects about a third more information than we need. If you already know it, or you know where to access it, you can throw the paper away.

Keep the new-information pile, and take careful note of the things that spark new ideas. You can store this information manually, in your filing cabinet or electronically in OneNote or Evernote for easy retrieval.

Did you know that only about 5 percent of people who promise something to an editor or agent at a conference actually follow through? In order to make sure you are in the 5 percent, you will need to make a plan and work the plan.

Find ways to make yourself accountable:

- Use social media to express what you've learned at the conference. Your connections will soon become your cheering section as you make new inroads to your goals.

- Join a critique group. If you belong to a writers association, check with your coordinators. Groups may already be looking for new members. If not, consider starting your own critique group.

- Buy the books you discovered during the conference.

- Finish writing thank-you notes to editors, agents, and people who added value to your writing during the conference.

Use your calendar to create success:

Great coaches tell us that when we think about something, it becomes a dream. When we focus on something, it becomes a possibility. When we plan something, it becomes probable, but when we put it on our calendars, it happens.

- Make a list of everything you promised.

- Schedule time on your calendar to fulfill those promises within sixty days.

Let's say you had one editor who was interested in your book proposal, and another who liked your pitch on an article. How much time will you need to complete these projects? When is your best writing time? Block out that time on your calendar and designate what you will work on each day.

Create

You've made the plan, but now you have to walk it. Take time at the beginning of each week to review your calendar, and then work your plan. By the end of sixty days, you will have not only delivered on your promises, but you will also have deepened your relationships with editors, agents, and other writers.

*   *   *

Kim Martinez *is an ordained Assemblies of God pastor with a Masters in Theology degree from Fuller Seminary. She is a ministry and life-development coach and can be found online at* www.deepimprints.com *and* www.getunstuckbootcamp.com. *She writes a weekly column for* ministrytodaymag.com.

*   *   *

🕐 For Further Coaching:

All full links to author websites, articles and blog posts are provided at http://www.nwchristianwriters.org/

- ✓ Nick Harrison, Senior Editor at Harvest House Publishers, published *"It's a Lot of Little Steps."*

- ✓ *"A Model of the Creative Process"* was posted by Dubberly Design Office.

- ✓ Hartline Literary Agency blogged *"After the Conference"* by Andy Scheer.

- ✓ *"How to Be Organized"* on WikiHow to Do Anything.

- ✓ Davalynn Spencer guest blogged *"Bunny Trails or How to Stay on Track"* on Word Sharpeners.

- ✓ *"Don't Let Your Ideas Rot, Germinate Them"* on the Sebastian Marshall website.

- ✓ *"After the Conference: Putting it All Together"* posted by Lindy Jacobs, Director of the Oregon Christian Writers (OCW) Summer Conference on her website Lindy Jacobs: Writer at the Well.

Appendix A – Resources

You can find all the links in this book in one place:

http://www.nwchristianwriters.org/Conferences

Interested in learning more about the organization that developed this book?

The Northwest Christian Writers Association is a group of writers and speakers in the Seattle area.

We join together at monthly meetings, our annual conference, and special events to learn the craft, grow in faith, and encourage one another.

If you're interested in learning more about faith based writing and speaking, NCWA offers:

- A speakers bureau

- A bi-monthly newsletter

- A blog

- Resource recommendations

Learn more about these and our members at:

www.nwchristianwriters.org

You will also find great books on writing and many of the books written by our authors at:

http://astore.amazon.com/northchriswri-20

You will find more resources at:

http://www.nwchristianwriters.org/SuggestedResources

Appendix B: Meet the Authors and Contributors

Lynnette Bonner

Born and raised in Malawi, Africa, Lynnette Bonner spent the first years of her life reveling in warm equatorial sunshine and the late evening duets of cicadas and hyenas. The year she turned eight she was off to Rift Valley Academy, a boarding school in Kenya where she spent many joy-filled years, and graduated in 1990.

That fall, she traded to a new duet--one of traffic and rain--when she moved to Kirkland, Washington to attend Northwest University. It was there that she met her husband and a few years later they moved to the small town of Pierce, Idaho.

During the time they lived in Idaho, while studying the history of their little town, Lynnette was inspired to begin the *Shepherd's Heart Series* with *Rocky Mountain Oasis*.

Marty and Lynnette have four children, and currently live in Washington where Marty pastors a church. You can find Lynnette online at www.lynnettebonner.com.

Delora Buoy

Delora A. Buoy's most recent endeavor was working on the e-book, Christian Writer's Coach: Conferences, as line-editor and serving on the Planning Committee – a project she thoroughly enjoyed and found exciting. She has been published in Christian Communicator, Journeys in Prayer, Northwest Christian Author, and Ozarks Chapter of American Christian Writers' newsletter. In these publications, she wrote feature stories, profiles, some how-to's, and some essays.

She has been a contributing member of The Christian PEN: Proofreaders and Editors Network and has written editor profiles for its online newsletter, PEN Points.

For eight-plus years, Delora was proofreader for The UPC Times, a bimonthly newspaper for a Seattle mega-church. Therein, she wrote numerous feature/ profile articles, writing of trials and triumphs of Christians in that fellowship – stories crying out to be told.

She loves the wordsmithing process of line-editing to make manuscripts more readable, more polished and correct in grammar and style – in other words, to help get the writer's points across.

Additionally, she was chief editor one year for the annual publication of Seattle Central Community College's Women's Programs, titled Women's Forum.

Delora was a member of Toastmasters International for over four years and earned two awards.

Dennis Brooke

Dennis Brooke was fired from his first writing job—as the editor for his junior high newspaper. Since then he has written for *Focus on the Family*, *Combat Crew*, and *Toastmaster* magazines as well as dozens of local and trade publications. His manuscript, *The Last Apostle,* was a finalist in the Marcher Lord Press Select contest and semi-finalist in the American Christian Fiction Writers Genesis contest. He teaches on storytelling, speaking, technology, and leadership topics.

Dennis is a former Air Force officer who served in Germany where he was blessed to witness the fall of the Berlin Wall—and got to spend one day as a spy. He now manages information technology projects in locales ranging from Sydney to Sault St. Marie. He can often be found on his bike or kayak exploring God's creation.

Dennis' passion is using the power of storytelling to influence people and organizations. He currently serves as President of the Northwest Christian Writers Association and tells stories at www.dennisbrooke.com

Kathleen Freeman

Kathleen knew writing was in her future the day her third grade teacher discovered that instead of learning how to multiply double digits, she was writing a poem... and praised her. However, knowing it was difficult to make a living as a writer, she decided she had better be a teacher and a writer, or a marine biologist and a writer, a counselor and a writer—a brain surgeon and a writer. Now, she does all these things, except the brain surgery, which she avoids, even on a volunteer basis. Kathleen spends her days working on novels and articles, researching, editing, and encouraging those around her to grow their writing. Her work appears in Vista Journal for Holy Living, the NCWA Newsletter, Raising Small Souls, and Clubhouse Magazine.

Kathleen was the 2012 Genesis winner for the YA category, has several completed novels, and a number of works in progress. You can find her online at findinghopeinhardtimes.com.

Lydia Harris

Lydia E. Harris, M.A. in home economics, has contributed to 18 books and has written hundreds of articles, devotionals, book reviews, and personal-experience stories since she began writing in 1998. Her bimonthly column, "A Cup of Tea with Lydia," appears in the *Country Register* papers in the United States and Canada with a readership of nearly 3/4 million. (No wonder her grandkids call her "Grandma Tea.") Focus on the Family's *Clubhouse* magazines for children publish her recipes, which she develops and tests with her grandchildren.

Lydia has also written a Bible study, *Preparing My Heart for Grandparenting*, which is based on years of teaching and grandparenting. It's available through the author and several Internet sites, such as amazon.com.

As a frequent speaker and conference teacher, Lydia shares on topics she is passionate about: grandparenting, hospitali-TEA, and prayer. She has prayed weekly with other mothers, and now grandmothers, for more than twenty years.

Together, Lydia and her husband, Milt of forty-five years are intentional about passing on a legacy of faith to their two married children and five grandchildren. You can contact Lydia at LydiaHarrisbooks@Gmail.com.

Michelle Hollomon

Michelle is a counselor, author, speaker and host of Relationship Coach Radio. She is wife to Mr. Dashing, mother of Sweet and *Sassy*, and tolerator of one naughty dog. Michelle's book *"God Unwrapped: God is Love but not the kind You're Used To"* is published by Harrison House. You can find her at http://www.michellehollomon.com/

Agnes Lawless

Author and copy editor Agnes Lawless Elkins has authored or coauthored eleven books, notably, The Drift into Deception (Kregel); Captivated by God (Gospel Light); Under His Wings (Christian Growth Ministries); and Keys to God's Heart: Unlocking Leviticus (Pleasant Word). She and her late husband, Richard E. Elkins, coauthored Time and Again: God's Sovereignty in the Lives of Two Bible Translators in the Philippines (WestBow).

Agnes's articles have been published in such magazines as Decision, Power for Living, Light and Life, Evangel, Live,

Christian Standard, and the Christian Communicator. She has had several articles published in anthologies. She also copyedits and proofreads books for publishers and individuals.

Agnes is a graduate of Seattle Pacific University and of Prairie Bible College. She did graduate work at Syracuse University in religious journalism. She was one of the founders of the Northwest Christian Writers Association and is the managing editor of its newsletter, Northwest Christian Author.

Amy Letinsky

Amy Letinsky is a college writing and literature instructor. She enjoys writing for many different circumstances, including writing for the web, newspaper and magazine journalism, and research based essays. Amy has been published by MOPS' MomSense Magazine and Focus on the Family's Thriving Family Magazine. Personal essays are her favorite form of writing, but she also writes some short stories and is working on a couple of non-fiction book projects. Although she wrote a novel for NaNoWriMo a few years ago, she continues to edit it and wonders if she'll ever be happy with it.

Reading and studying great literature is fundamental to Amy's success as a writer. Her academic studies focus on British literature, especially the work of John Milton and John Bunyan. Jane Austen holds a special place in her heart as well. She draws inspiration from many types of authors and continually challenges herself to read new and different books.

Amy lives in the Seattle area with her husband Daniel and her two young daughters. Follow her adventures in parenting and the writing life at her blog <u>amyletinsky.wordpress.com</u>.

Kim Martinez

Kim is a pastor, coach, writer and serves on the board of Northwest Christian Writers Association. You will find her online at <u>www.deepimprints.com</u>. Recently, she developed a four-week webinar that you can find at <u>www.getunstuckbootcamp.com</u>. Kim has a weekly column at <u>www.ministrytodaymag.com</u>. She also has her Masters in Theology from Fuller Seminary, and is ordained with the Assemblies of God. In the rest of life, Kim has four kids – early teens to young adult – and a fantastic, creative husband, Wes.

Marlene McClurley

Marlene McCurley has done freelance copyediting, proofreading, and promotional writing for over twelve years. She has worked in Christian education support for nearly twenty years and is currently Program and Budget Manager for the College of Arts and Sciences at Seattle Pacific University. She has earned a BA in Sociology from Friends University in Wichita, Kansas and an Editing Certificate from the Graham School at the University of Chicago, the home of the Chicago Manual of Style. She has volunteered for the Western and Central Washington Chapter of the Alzheimer's Association and is a member of the Editorial Freelancers Association, the Northwest Independent Editors Guild, and the Northwest Christian Writers Association.

Marlene and her husband, Dennis, are members of Crossroads Bible Church and they have two married children and two practically perfect grandchildren. Besides having two jobs and being a busy wife, mom, and gran, Marlene is writing a memoir about the impact of Alzheimer's disease on her family. Her blog can be found at www.mwords.net/why.

Lesley Ann McDaniel

Born in Missoula, Montana, she was one of the original Dwarfs in the Missoula Children's Theatre's inaugural production of "Snow White", which is still touring the world.

While earning a degree in acting at Willamette University in Salem, Oregon, she fell in love with theatrical costuming, and pursued that as a career while nurturing her passion for writing on the side. Through God's guidance, she has shifted her focus to honing her skills as a writer of romance and young adult fiction.

Between working as a homeschooling mom and as a professional theatre costumer, Lesley has completed several novels. She would have done more by now if she didn't also occasionally stop to clean the house. Fortunately, she loves to cook, so no one in her family has starved yet.

She is a member of the Northwest Christian Writers Association, American Christian Fiction Writers, and a wonderful critique group. A native Montanan and a Big Sky girl at heart, Lesley now resides in the Seattle area with her husband, two daughters, three cats and a big loud dog. In her spare time (ha!) she chips away at her goal of reading every book ever written. Please visit her website at www.lesleyannmcdaniel.com.

Gigi Murfitt

Gigi Devine Murfitt writes and speaks about God's work in her life. Raised in a single parent home with nine siblings, her life has been dotted with stories of courage and hope.

Gigi has published several articles in newspapers, newsletters and magazines, including two stories in Guideposts Books compilation series – *Extraordinary Answers to Prayers.* She is author of *Caregivers' Devotions to Go (2010)* and co-author of *My Message is C.L.E.A.R. – Hope and Strength in the Face of Life's Greatest Adversities (2012)*

A lover of God's Word, Gigi has facilitated Bible study for many years. She has been a speaker at retreats and enjoys mentoring women in their walk of faith.

Gigi serves on the Board of Directors for the Northwest Christian Writers Association. She is a member of the Speaker's Connection.

The Murfitt family is often asked to share their incredible story. They have established a 501(c)3 nonprofit organization named "Gabriel's Foundation of HOPE". They encourage families dealing with disabilities by helping them overcome and persevere. www.GabesHOPE.org

Melissa Norris

Melissa K. Norris is an inspirational novelist, newspaper columnist, and blogger. A skilled artisan crafter, she creates new traditions from old-time customs for her readers. She found her own little house in the big woods, where she lives with her husband and two children in the Cascade Mountains. She writes a monthly column, Pioneering Today, for the local newspaper that bridges her love of the past with its usefulness in modern life. Her books and articles are inspired by her family's small herd of beef cattle, her amateur barrel racing days, and her forays into quilting and canning—without always reading the directions first. www.melissaknorris.com She is also co-owner of TriLink Social Media Mentors at www.trilink-social-media.com

Mindy Peltier

Mindy Peltier was a reporter and columnist for the Cavalier County Republican during high school in North Dakota. The picture of her in braces on the column header still follows her through life.

After college, she married Scott, and they had six children. Although she homeschooled them, she continued to write, even if it was only letters, fragmented story ideas, and grocery lists. After potty training the last child, she rewarded herself by using those precious extra minutes a day to write real stuff. She also began attending writers conferences and learning about the craft of writing.

Blogging has been her commitment to discipline herself as a writer and to discipline her family to let her write.

She has blogged over a thousand posts about her life as a Christian mom, grandma, thyroid-cancer patient, and writer at *In the Write Moment*.

Mindy loves serving with her husband as he ministers as an elder and a Bible camp preacher. She's a member of the Oregon Christian Writers as well as the Northwest Christian Writers Association and serves on the board of directors for (NCWA).

TriLink Social Media

TriLink Social Media Mentors specializes in helping publishing professionals discover, implement, and market their brands. Without a strong brand in place, all marketing and social media efforts fall short. In fact, neglected or inaccurate branding can have a negative impact on a career. TriLink Mentors Melissa K Norris and Janalyn Voigt partner with those ready to discover their brands, help take existing branding deeper, and customize plans to implement and market brands. They specialize in working with authors who need branding and social media made simple.

The business name derives from Ecclesiastes 4:12: "And if one can overpower him who is alone, two can resist him. A cord of three strands is not quickly torn apart" (NAS Bible). We conduct our business with one thing in mind: to allow God His rightful place in the center between us, exemplified in the TriLink logo by the larger circle between two smaller circles. We also believe the circles represent our clients, God, and ourselves. http://TriLink-Social-Media.com

Kim Vandel

Kim Vandel grew up on a steady diet of Sunday school lessons and Saturday morning Justice League cartoons, which might explain her love for stories that push the boundaries of faith and imagination.

She graduated summa cum laude from Northwest Nazarene University with a degree in biology and worked in an environmental testing lab before staying home to be a fulltime mom and writer. She now uses her science background to bring the speculative element of her YA fiction to life.

She's a member of Northwest Christian Writers Association and serves on the NCWA social media team. She's also a member of American Christian Fiction Writers and was a semi-finalist in their 2011 Genesis Contest.

Kim always has a book or two close by, and when she's not distracted with reading or writing fiction, she loves to blog about it. Join in the conversation at kimvandel.com.

Erica Vetsch

Erica is a transplanted Kansan now residing in Minnesota. She loves history and reading, and is blessed to be able to combine the two by writing historical fiction set in the American West. Whenever she's not following flights of fancy in her fictional world, she's the company bookkeeper for the family lumber business, mother of two terrific kids, wife to a man who is her total opposite and soul-mate, and avid museum patron. You can find her online at http://onthewritepath.blogspot.com/.

Janalyn Voigt

Janalyn Voigt serves as a literary judge for several national contests and is an active book reviewer. Her unique blend of adventure, romance, suspense, and fantasy creates worlds of beauty and danger for readers. Beginning with DawnSinger, Janalyn's epic fantasy series, *Tales of Faeraven*, carries the reader into a land only imagined in dreams. She also writes historical romance novels and is represented by Wordserve Literary.

Janalyn posts interesting details from her research, travel journals, and author journals at *Creative Worlds* and is one of 31 historical fiction novelists who join forces at the *Christian Fiction Historical Society* blog. At her *Live Write Breathe* site, Janalyn teaches authors to live with passion, write well, and remember to breathe. She also contributes to her agency's blog, *Wordserve Water Cooler*. Together with her business partner Melissa K. Norris, Janalyn mentors writers and other publishing professionals on branding at *TriLink Social Media Mentors* and through writing conferences. Janalyn is affiliated with American Christian Fiction Writers and Northwest Christian Writers Association.

When she's not writing, Janalyn loves to find adventures in the great outdoors. You can also follow her on *Facebook | Twitter | Google+ | Goodreads | Pinterest | Youtube* Author website: *Janalyn Voigt*